Enhancing Learning through Assessment in Business and Management, Hospitality, Leisure, Sport, Tourism

A valuable resource for academics/teachers committed to improving their learning and teaching, and ultimately, the learning outcomes for students. As is now well recognised, assessment drives student learning, and while the focus of this collection of papers is on assessment in Business and Management, Hospitality, Leisure, Sport and Tourism, the discussion, and in particular the excellent examples of current practice, provides a valuable resource for all those involved in teaching in higher education.

Associate Professor Kim Watty
Principal Research Fellow, Graduate School of Business
and Economics, University of Melbourne

This book opens a window onto assessment in the BMAF/HLST subject communities. It displays an interesting landscape, showing innovation and thoughtful assessment design as key features, and providing honest evaluations of practical issues and contextual challenges. It will be an inspiration for practitioners who wish to review and enhance their practice.

Margaret Price
Director of the ASKe CETL and Professor in Learning
and Assessment, Oxford Brookes University

Edited by Patsy Kemp, Richard Atfield and
Richard Tong

Enhancing
Learning through Assessment
in Business and Management
Hospitality
Leisure
Sport
Tourism

Threshold Press

First published 2010 by
Threshold Press Ltd
152 Craven Road
Newbury Berks RG14 5NR
Phone 01635-230272 and fax 01635-44804
email: publish@threshold-press.co.uk
www.threshold-press.co.uk

British Library Cataloguing in Publication Data
A catalogue record for this book is available from the British Library

ISBN 978–1–903152–25–6

Printed in England by MPG Biddles Ltd, Kings Lynn

Every effort has been made to trace the copyright holders and we apologise in
advance for any unintentional omissions. The editors and the publisher would be
pleased to insert the appropriate acknowledgement in any subsequent edition.

The editors

Patsy Kemp has experience of working in education and training across the globe. As
academic developments co-ordinator for the Higher Education Academy Network
for Hospitality, Leisure, Sport & Tourism, she works to support practitioners in
their roles in higher education.

Richard Atfield is assistant director for the Business Management Accountancy and
Finance Subject Centre. He is responsible for facilitating workshops, special interest groups and other learning opportunities, including the 2010 BMAF Conference
on 'Assessment and Assessment Standards'. His career spans management and
workforce development in the NHS and lecturing in the UK and Hong Kong for
Oxford Brookes University.

Richard Tong is the director of learning & teaching and deputy dean in the Cardiff
School of Sport at UWIC. He is also the sport liaison officer for the HE Academy
Subject Centre for Hospitality, Leisure, Sport and Tourism. He is the chair of the
Education & Professional Development Division for the British Association of
Sport & Exercise Science and the moderator champion for learning & teaching
for the University of Wales. His research interests and publications are in sports
physiology, pedagogy and assessment.

Contents

Editors' Foreword

Patsy Kemp, Richard Atfield and Richard Tong

In 2006, the two Higher Education Academy subject centres representing business, management, accountancy and finance, and hospitality, leisure, sport and tourism, decided to collect and publish case studies in which practitioners wrote for practitioners, sharing stories of enhancing employability at their universities. This book became the first in a series using the same case study format, enabling our communities to explore themes current in higher education and reveal the lessons they felt they had learned from their experiences. The next two books, published in 2008 and 2009, covered international learning and student centred learning.

It had long been in our minds that assessment was an issue we should put forward as part of this 'enhancing' series of books. Assessment is such an important element in the experience of both staff and students and debate has been growing over how assessment can be used to engage students in learning – assessment for learning rather than assessment of learning. Professor Mantz Yorke, in his introductory chapter talks of 'the tension between assessment as support of learning and as a means of certifying student achievement', and this tension is integral to the book. Written by those working directly in learning and teaching for the benefit of their peers, the book weaves together themes which illustrate some of the difficulties of resolving this tension, in a variety of contexts and with a range of approaches.

The first and final case studies come from two CETLs: Assessment Standards Knowledge exchange (ASKe) in Oxford Brookes University and Assessment for Learning (AfL) in Northumbria University. They both highlight the positive impact on learning that engaging students in the process of assessment brings. Allin and Fishwick (Northumbria) showcase an undergraduate Sport Development degree which has adopted a programme-led approach to assessment. O'Donovan (Oxford Brookes Business School) talks of creating an 'assessment literate' learning community which contains students who share an understanding of assessment with staff, and who are actively engaged with assessment standards.

The themes of employability and the workplace also run through the book. Work-based learning is directly discussed by two of the case studies, with Beattie at Liverpool John Moores using e-portfolios to develop competences in sports students and Hummel in Heidelberg looking at the nature of assessment strategies and standards for 'live' or real world consulting projects in hospitality.

The world of work and its needs thread through several other chapters. Reedy and Mordaunt at the Open University find that new technologies can help in the assessment of some of the difficult skills needed in the workplace, such as collaborative learning. Gordon, then at Queen Margaret University, Edinburgh, discusses the practical introduction of e-portfolios, and the skills of planning and reflection which students must develop to achieve success both with their portfolios and at work. Rushton, Sparshatt and O'Brien at Sheffield Hallam use formative feedback to support students in the acquisition of transferable skills such as research or analysis. Group work, group processes and peer learning feature – from very different angles – in the case studies of Canterbury Christ Church (Garratt) and University of Westminster/London Metropolitan (Pokorny and Griffiths); the former aims to share assessment practices that engage culturally diverse postgraduate students in team working and thus help them appreciate their peers; the latter explores the complexities – and value – of group work assessment practices, with staff paralleling the student experience. Lean and Moizer from the University of Plymouth Business School use oral de-briefing to encourage good reflection on the 'virtual' workplace experience of a computer-based business simulation game, as well as considering the challenges of assessing student learning using this approach.

All the case studies contain some element of innovation – be it technological or methodological – for the writers and their institutions, and introduce us to innovations in practice. Anderson's chapter (Southampton Solent) looks at the development of inclusive assessment methods not fully dependent on the written word; the chapter by Thomas and Tong of the University of Wales Institute, Cardiff (UWIC) investigates an innovative way of managing student dissertations in a complex modular system; Baker at the University of the West of England reflects on the key issues arising from the introduction of a new programme of assessment allowing students to gain from meaningful formative feedback. Neil, Wilson and Tong's case study (UWIC) contains both technological and methodological innovation – it deals with electronic submission of assessment in sport-related research, and explains how feedback was targeted and individualised for each student.

The research carried out by Hatzipanagos at King's Learning Institute, King's College London, highlights again the tension between supporting and measuring learning; those involved in distance learning, where the research took place, have been some of those at the forefront of developing formative assessment systems as they cannot easily give feedback any other way. This chapter shares the research done on how far formative assessment activities are used to improve learning, and how this is perceived by tutors and students.

We acknowledge with gratitude Professor Mantz Yorke who has provided an introductory chapter which deliberates on and extends the issues raised by the authors. We thank all those who have worked hard to provide us with the case studies. We hope that this collection will provide food for thought and debate among the business, management, accountancy and finance, and hospitality, leisure, sport and tourism communities that provided it, and that some of its messages will be relevant and useful further afield.

Introduction:
Assessing emergent professional expertise

Mantz Yorke

Professional expertise, rather than 'skills'

A key aim of programmes in hospitality, leisure, sport and tourism [HLST], and in business, management, accounting and finance [BMAF] is that graduates should, in one way or another, develop their expertise as professionals in the world of work. While some may see this as indicative of a narrow instrumentalism, it implies the combination of traditional academic values associated with learning and capabilities aligned with specific areas of employment. It is a case of 'both/and' rather than 'either/or'. And higher education traditionalists should not forget that the Robbins Report (Committee on Higher Education, 1963) placed the relationship between academy and the national economy first in its four aims for higher education lest it be overlooked. However, the Robbins Committee seems to have been too optimistic on this point.

In more recent times, governmental policy in the UK has stressed the acquisition of skills, qualifying 'skills' with adjectives such as 'core', 'transferable' and 'generic'. The emphasis on skills has lacked a substantive rationale, as Wolf (2002) has demonstrated, and – from an academic point of view at least – seems little more than a political mantra that seems to be continually recycled in official documents such as the Leitch Report (2006).

The Enhancing Student Employability Co-ordination Team [ESECT] was concerned in its work to avoid the negative connotations of 'skills', and stressed in its USEM formulation of employability the importance of skilful practices in context (Yorke and Knight, 2006). This choice of terminology embraces the 'integrativity' of action, drawing – as appropriate to the circumstances – on personal repertoires in the cognitive, affective and psychomotor domains. It is this 'integrativity' that poses significant challenges for assessment practices that, too often, are legacies from scientific approaches to measurement. Amongst the issues involved are:

❑ the purposes of assessment
❑ standards
❑ assessment methodology
❑ assessors' capabilities
❑ the relationship between theory and practice.

There is space in this introduction for only a few compass bearings relevant to the terrain, rather than a fully worked-out route map. The compass bearings that are offered have been influenced by the following chapters, and the reader will be able to pick up echoes of themes that they contain.

The purposes of assessment

In a number of the chapters in this book there is a tension between two main roles for assessment – in support of learning, and as a means of certifying students' achievements. The two roles are fundamentally different, yet are often smudged together on the same metaphorical piece of paper.

Assessment for learning is (tautologically) formative. It not only points out errors and weaknesses, but also what students might do to improve their performance in respect of subsequent assessment tasks – its 'feed-forward' function. One of the challenges for higher education is to ensure that students respond positively to commentaries on their work that point to ways in which they can develop their capabilities. Too often, it seems, students simply glance at the grade and put the assignment aside, obviating the formative purpose of tutors' comments. The problem has at least three components:

❏ Structural, in that feedback arrives too late to be useful (or to be perceived as useful), though podcasting is being used by some in an attempt to make feedback more rapid and perhaps more accessible.
❏ A narrow instrumentalism adopted by students ('the grade's the thing, and especially so if it can get me over the 2.2 / 2.1 boundary').
❏ A more broadly cultural dimension connected to point 2 above, in that the achievement of expected outcomes is often accorded more attention than wider learning. This is a by-product of too tight a curricular 'constructive alignment' (Biggs and Tang, 2007) and the perceived need to exhibit robustness in quality assurance, and is also of some influence where 'league tables' of institutions factor the proportion of first and upper second class degrees awarded into their orderings.

Summative assessment provides a record, for students, employers and other interested parties, of the level of achievement reached in an assignment or a whole programme. Those inside higher education know that summative grades are referenced against disciplinary norms, irrespective of the extent to which the actual assessments are criterion-referenced. A glance at the statistics published by the Higher Education Statistics Agency shows how the pattern of honours degree awards varies with subject area (and only part of that variation can be attributed to variation in institutional enrolment).

Many assessments at the level of the course component serve both summative and formative functions. Module grades, for example, are cumulated into an overall index of achievement, but the commentaries on the work are expected to serve a formative function. The summative aspect may lead some students to be reluctant to take risks with their learning: better to go for the 'safe' 2.1 than to go all out but risk getting a low grade. A higher education worthy of the name should surely encourage students to reach the highest point they can, but should not penalise unduly those whose reach turns out to have exceeded their grasp. The point arises particularly sharply in respect of work-based learning, where a student may not have been particularly successful in the actual workplace but has learned a great deal from the experience. Reflective commentary on experience may indicate that the learning might well be converted into a more successful practical performance on a future occasion. To what extent, then, should (summative) weakness be redeemed by (formative) success?

Standards

There is plenty of evidence that that the articulation of academic standards is less precise than many would prefer to be the case, despite attempts to frame them; for example, through the subject benchmark statements compiled by the Quality Assurance Agency (QAA). Normative understandings of what is expected develop over time in subject communities, and continue to evolve as the subjects and pedagogic methodologies themselves evolve. Assessment criteria, likewise, present a challenge. For national vocational qualifications (NVQs) the solution advocated by Jessup (1991), following in the footsteps of Mager (1962), was to try to pin down achievements against tightly-stated criteria. While the approach might have been of some conceptual merit in the context of a narrowly-conceived skills curriculum, in practice its rigidity was necessarily softened at the higher levels of NVQ-based curricula. At the higher NVQ levels, the 'skills' tended towards being managerial and 'generic', implying a need to cater in the assessment process for students' contextually-driven interpretations, judgements and actions.

The assessment of 'generic skills' or what Knight and Page (2007: 2) called 'wicked' competences (i.e. achievements that cannot be neatly pre-specified, take time to develop and resist measurement based approaches to assessment) is very challenging. But before one gets to considerations of the actual assessment methodology, the codification of expected learning outcomes and standards is likewise challenging. In a discussion document, the Australian Universities Quality Agency would seem to have been attracted by the temptation to try to specify, in considerable detail, standards and levels of performance:

> Introducing standardised and understood methods of assessing and grading these [generic] attributes, at the level of difficulty appropriate to the stage of the learning process, ensures that students better understand why they must learn particular things and also provides meaningful evidence to use as part of their future career activities (AUQA, 2009: 12).

The document seems to have overlooked the contextual specificity of the environment in which the performance has been achieved – for example, business settings vary considerably and hence what can be achieved cannot be standardised. What can be done is to set out a set of broad expectations and, in effect, ask the student to respond to the question: 'How have you satisfied, through your work, the aims stated for your programme of study?' (Yorke, 1998: 181).

The same question can be asked of a curriculum component, such as work-based experience. Summative assessment then becomes a matter of *judgement* as to the extent to which the student has achieved what was expected. The judgement may be on a pass/fail basis, or with reference to broad bands: finely-grained scales, such as the so-called 'percentage scale' ('Percentage of what?' is always a difficult question to answer), are less appropriate. While some might be concerned at the coarseness of the judgements, a study based on real assessment data shows that, across a whole programme, it may not make much difference whether a coarse or fine scale is used (Yorke, forthcoming).

In higher education, where students are expected to exercise independence in respect of their studies, the situation regarding learning outcomes and assessment criteria has a parallel with the fairy-tale of *Goldilocks and the three bears*. Outcomes and criteria have to be expressed in an optimal way – neither too tightly nor too loosely. The trouble is that optimality is elusive, and essentially a matter of judgement within the academic community. The ASKe Centre for Excellence in Teaching and Learning has argued that an understanding of standards (and, by extension, outcomes and criteria) depends on collegial discussion within the relevant academic community (ASKe, 2008). But what is the 'relevant academic community', when the subject area concerned embraces a number of disciplines, as do most of the HLST and BMAF subjects? 'Community', for these subjects (and many others) may have to be viewed in open system terms, rather than with reference to hermetically-sealed disciplines.

Statements of learning outcomes and assessment criteria are insufficient to convey what the expectations laid on students really are, as is evident from a slew of sources including Wolf (1995), Price and Rust (1999), Rust et al. (2003), and O'Donovan et al. (2004). Exemplification is the key to the conveying of meaning. A survey of assessment practices currently being conducted for a guide to be published by Foundation Degree Forward is showing that a number of programmes offer examples of assignments on the relevant website in order that students can more readily appreciate what standard of work is being expected of them.

Some observations on assessment methodology

From the perspective of assessment for learning, a major issue is that of how to secure student engagement, in order that students do not simply address their tasks in order to gain a level of pass with which they will be satisfied. A commitment to 'learning goals' is needed. This is where negotiation between staff and students about assessment tasks, ranging from the involvement of students in the design of assessments to the formalisation of learning contracts, has a part to play. Programmes with elements of work-based or work-related learning have considerable potential for fostering student engagement in this way. Note, though, that this embraces the context-specificity mentioned earlier, with its implication that commonality of standards can only be achieved in broad terms.

Employment-oriented programmes necessarily include the development of capabilities relating to working with others. Group-work offers a way of realising this potential, but not without difficulties. Mark Lejk and various co-workers have been prominent in exploring the assessment of group-work through a number of articles (see, for example, Lejk and Wyvill, 2002). Lejk (2008) has examined the social aspects of assessing group-work, including the challenges associated with having culturally diverse groups and with 'free-riding'. As management consultants are wont to say, the challenges can be seen as learning opportunities, since people have to deal with their analogues in the workplace. Assessment tasks might, therefore, incorporate analysis of the dynamics associated with group-work, and an indication of the lessons learned that might be put to good use in an employment context.

Reflection has become a staple of assessment, especially in respect of learning from workplace experience where it often forms a component of portfolios. Student reaction is mixed: some have been concerned that self-criticism might encourage an assessor towards awarding a lower grade than might otherwise be the case; others have seen reflection as 'a waste of time'. Yet self-assessment is an essential component of learning, whether it be informal or formalised through an assessment schedule. The ability to self-assess is an important aspect of the autonomy that various writers on student development (though typically with young undergraduates in mind) assert as a fundamental issue for higher education. A recent example is given by Baxter Magolda (2009: 144) who writes (using slightly different terminology) that

> Guiding learners through the transformation from authority dependence to self-authorship is a primary challenge for twenty-first-century higher education.

Many mature entrants to higher education have already developed substantial personal autonomy, and their primary developmental needs may lie elsewhere.

Assessors' capabilities

Assessors are generally confident about their ability to assess student work within their subject discipline. Knight and Page (2007) found that when it came to assessing 'wicked' competences – for example, oral communication and the development of supportive relationships – the level of confidence amongst a sample of 83 colleagues from the Open University was similarly high. The reasons for this latter confidence were unclear, but may have included an element of 'I know it when I see it' born of experience in the relevant field. This would imply a capacity to judge when students are meeting criteria that may be partly implicit and partly explicit – as would be expected of assessors who have relevant experience of employment. Such judgements are more difficult to make when the assessor lacks workplace experience – indeed, it is a bit like assessing in a foreign language in which one has limited fluency.

Assessment in employment-focused subjects such as those in HLST and BMAF typically involves employers in some way. Evidence from foundation degrees suggests that, while employers might be willing to assess on a pass/fail basis (or to attest to the development of specified competences, where there are defined occupational standards), they are less willing to grade more finely. There are various reasons for this, amongst them the conflict of interest between the roles of mentor and assessor. However, academic assignments are typically graded in some way, and the overall grade for the programme as a whole is determined by the grading for the academic achievements and not the workplace-based achievements. In bachelor's degree programmes, the workplace achievements are often represented by proxy – through some form of commentary on the experience which is intended to be reflective in nature. If it counts towards the overall award for the programme, the weighting is usually vestigial.

The differential between the academic achievements and those derived from the workplace raises, in an oblique form, the issue of the relationship between theory and practice.

The relationship between theory and practice

Like a leitmotif that returns in a different key in an orchestral work, an exploration of the relationship between theory and practice brings with it a return to the issue of the purposes of assessment. A traditional perspective on higher education is that students should 'learn the theory' in their academic studies before putting it into actual practice in the workplace. Some kinds of programme do not exhibit such linearity: for instance, nursing, social work and teacher education are three subjects in which the theoretical and practical are interspersed. Foundation degrees, too, are expected to bring the academic and the practical close together.

Programmes that are non-linear, as far as the way that students engage with theory and practice is concerned, implicitly acknowledge the 'messiness' of many challenges in the world outside higher education. There are, of course, pockets of ordering where practices are – for some time, at least – taken as 'givens' and not subjected to critical scrutiny. A student has to respond acceptably to these orderings (which could be occupational standards or prescribed competences) in order to gain the qualification that is being sought. Changes to accepted practices are usually incremental and evolutionary, rather than revolutionary. It is rather as Otto Neurath's metaphor has it: we replace the rotting timbers of our ship, one by one, as it sails along, trusting the while in the structural integrity of the remainder, cited by Popper (1972: 60). Or, taking a different tack, we use existing tools in order to achieve our objectives until we come across better ones and/or revise our objectives – the similarity with Argyris and Schön's (1974) single- and double-loop learning is palpable.

The social dimension to assessment

The enthusiasm of the writers of the various chapters in this book comes through clearly. A significant task for enthusiasts is to gain a sufficiently large band of support for the embedding of practices. While it may be relatively easy to pilot an innovation, the 'scalability' of the innovation to larger numbers presents a number of challenges, both social and organisational: Fullan (2001) has pointed convincingly to the social complexity inherent in obtaining 'buy-in' to innovation.

The challenge of innovating in assessment is all the more severe in a climate of resource constraint, and where institutions are advancing expectations relating to research and entrepreneurial activity simultaneously with those relating to 'the student experience'. A reality check as regards assessment is necessary: the benefit/cost ratio of introducing new assessment methods has to be noticeably greater than unity for assessors (whether this is determined quantitatively or qualitatively). The question 'What is in it for staff if they were to adopt different assessment practices' has to have a convincing positive response.

Then how might students respond to change in assessment methodology? They may not welcome innovation unless they are convinced that what is proposed is in their interests. Putting oneself in a similar position to students can be quite a salutary experience as regards the acceptability of an assessment method, as academics enrolled on study programmes often attest.

Some broader issues

Where there is a workplace element in a programme, it may (but does not necessarily) imply the student entering an experiential learning cycle such as that of Kolb (1984) at a different point from when they are engaging in academic studies. Where there is a difference in starting-point, there are implicit consequences for assessment. 'Academic learning' may be a consequence of 'practical learning', rather than vice versa. Hence consideration needs to be given to the way tasks are specified and performances assessed. The integrative potential of academic and workplace learning in a programme may only be realised fully as the student comes to its end – which would align with the view that assessment should have a 'whole programme' perspective . The 'capstone' project or dissertation is a (well-known) vehicle through which students may demonstrate learning derived from across their programme.

If the assessment of workplace achievements is predominantly a matter of professional judgement:

❑ How should workplace achievements be graded?
❑ How should summative grades for workplace achievements be integrated into the determination of the level of the relevant award (e.g. the classification of honours degrees)?
❑ How can the standards achieved in workplace settings be assured (e.g. through external examining and/or moderation)?

These questions are not straightforward to answer, since the answers have to reflect the social/educational environments within which assessment takes place. If practices need to be changed, then achieving change may not be easy. The Burgess Group's work on the honours degree classification implicitly indicates how difficult it has been to abandon a practice that was initially deemed to be no longer fit for purpose (compare UUK and SCoP, 2004 with UUK and GuildHE, 2007).

Yet, if higher education is to accept the implications of the longstanding expectation regarding its relationship with the national economy, a significant focus for change has to be assessment. Current practices are not always close to ideal, even with the innovation and pedagogic research that enthusiasts have pursued. If the metaphor of changing the direction of an oil tanker is applicable to educational change in general, then in respect of assessment a more appropriate metaphor might be that of attempting to divert a converging asteroid's trajectory, though it has to be admitted that failure would not be quite as disastrous.

References

Argyris, C. and Schön, D.A. (1974) *Theory in practice: increasing professional effectiveness*. San Francisco, CA: Jossey-Bass

ASKe (2008) Memorandum submitted to the Innovation, Universities, Science and Skills Committee in respect of its investigation into Students and Universities [Memorandum SU 09]. At www.publications.parliament.uk/pa/cm200809/cmselect/cmdius/memo/170/170memo0902.pdf (accessed 25 April 2010).

AUQA (2009) Setting and monitoring academic standards for Australian higher education (Discussion paper). At www.auqa.edu.au/qualityenhancement/academicstandards/discussion-paper.pdf (accessed 28 April 2010)

Baxter Magolda, M. (2009) Educating students for self-authorship: learning partnerships to achieve complex outcomes. In C. Kreber (ed) *The university and its disciplines: teaching and learning within and beyond disciplinary boundaries*. Abingdon: Routledge, pp. 143–56

Biggs, J. and Tang, C. (2007) *Teaching for quality learning at university* (3rd ed). Maidenhead: SRHE and Open University Press

Committee on Higher Education (1963) *Higher education [Report of the Committee appointed by the Prime Minister under the chairmanship of Lord Robbins, 1961–63]*. London: Her Majesty's Stationery Office

Fullan, M. (2001) *The new meaning of educational change* (3rd ed). New York: Teachers' College Press

Jessup, G. (1991) *Outcomes: NVQs and the emerging model of education and training*. London: Falmer

Knight, P. and Page, A. (2007) The assessment of 'wicked' competences. At www.open.ac.uk/cetl-workspace/cetlcontent/documents/460d21bd645f8.pdf (accessed 25 April 2010)

Kolb, D. A. (1984) *Experiential learning: experience as the source of learning and development*. Englewood Cliffs, NJ: Prentice-Hall

Leitch, S. (2006) *Prosperity for all in the global economy – world class skills [Final Report of the Leitch Review of Skills]*. Norwich: Her Majesty's Stationery Office

Lejk, E. (2008) Management of cultural diversity in group assessment for learning. At www.northumbria.ac.uk/static/5007/cetlpdf/emmaleyk pdf (accessed 26 April 2010)

Lejk, M and Wyvill, M. (2002) Peer assessment of contributions to a group project: student attitudes to holistic and category-based approaches. *Assessment and Evaluation in Higher Education* 27 (6) pp. 569–77

Mager, R. F. (1962) *Preparing instructional objectives*. Palo Alto, CA: Fearon

Popper, K. (1972) *Objective knowledge*. Oxford: Oxford University Press

O'Donovan, B., Price, M. and Rust, C. (2004) Know what I mean? Enhancing student understanding of assessment standards and criteria. *Teaching in Higher Education* 9 (3) pp. 325–35

Price, M. and Rust, C. (1999) The experience of introducing a common assessment grid across an academic department. *Quality in Higher Education* 5 (2) pp. 133–44

Rust, C., Price, M. and O'Donovan, B. (2003) Improving students' learning by developing their understanding of assessment criteria and processes. *Assessment and Evaluation in Higher Education* 28 (2) pp. 147–64

UUK and GuildHE (2007) *Beyond the honours degree classification: the Burgess Group final report*. London: Universities UK and GuildHE

UUK and SCoP (2004) *Measuring and recording student achievement*. London: Universities UK and Standing Conference of Principals

Wolf, A. (1995) *Competence-based assessment*. Buckingham: Open University Press

Wolf, A. (2002) *Does education matter? Myths about education and economic growth*. London: Penguin

Yorke, M. (1998) Assessing capability. In J. Stephenson and M. Yorke (eds) *Capability and quality in higher education*. London: Kogan Page pp. 174–91

Yorke, M. (forthcoming) How finely-grained does summative assessment need to be? *Studies in Higher Education*

Yorke, M. and Knight, P. (2006) *Embedding employability into the curriculum*. York: The Higher Education Academy

MANTZ YORKE spent six years as a senior manager at Liverpool Polytechnic followed by two years on secondment as Director of Quality Enhancement at the Higher Education Quality Council. He returned to his institution in 1994, continuing as Professor of Higher Education. Following retirement in 2005, he is Visiting Professor in the Department of Educational Research, Lancaster University. He was part of the Enhancing Student Employability Co-ordination Team (ESECT) project which led to his general editorship of the Learning and Employability series of publications by the Higher Education Academy. In addition to working on employability, he has researched, presented and published on various aspects of higher education, including the first year experience, retention and assessment.

Cultivating a community of assessment practice to enhance students' academic performance

Berry O' Donovan
Business School, Oxford Brookes University

How a community can support effective assessment and feedback practices, in particular, by sharing understandings of 'quality' in terms of students' assessed work. This chapter describes an attempt to cultivate a community of assessment practice that involves both staff and students.

Introduction

Assessment Standards Knowledge exchange (ASKe) is a Centre for Excellence in Teaching and Learning, funded by HEFCE, focused on sharing and communicating assessment understandings, particularly the often largely tacit perceptions of assessment standards.

ASKe is a centre for excellence in assessment, so for many colleagues ASKe's focus on cultivating community seems curious or even off track. However, an indispensable condition for students to do well in academic assessment is for them to hold the same conceptions of quality as that of their tutors (Rust et al, 2003; Sadler, 2009).

The nature of 'excellence' in a business report, essay, or dissertation is frustratingly difficult to articulate unambiguously and clearly. A number of issues block clear communication, including different interpretations of particular qualities or criteria. For example, if ten individuals are asked explicitly to define 'criticality' or 'analysis' it is likely that we will end up with ten different definitions, and the more diverse the group (nationality, educational experience etc) the more diverse the interpretations (O'Donovan et al, 2004).

Even more difficult is the unambiguous articulation of 'standards'. How do we describe the difference, say, between 'good' analysis at undergraduate and postgraduate level? When we make the attempt we fall back on relative terms, such as 'deeper', 'more complex', or the amount of student autonomy involved in the achievement. Such relative terms in turn require articulation of the benchmarks or anchor points to which they refer. So, we often end up with explanations which are too cumbersome and overly detailed for clear communication, merely attaining precision over practical utility which is 'likely to prove counter-productive' (Yorke, 2002: 155).

Difficulties notwithstanding, we reiterate, if students are to improve their academic performance we must communicate understandings of quality in terms of criteria and standards.

Tacit understandings of assessment standards and criteria (those parts of understanding that we find difficult to articulate in words) are personally shared through social processes, involving practice, observation and imitation. This is achieved more effectively in close academic communities where the density of interactions between students with staff, staff with staff and students with students is enhanced. So it is perhaps not surprising that large-scale research (involving 25,000 students and over 300 institutions) in the US found that the environmental variable which is the most significant predictor of student academic success is student involvement, as fostered by staff and peer interaction (Astin, 1993).

Prior research also points to the importance of a relational assessment environment to student academic performance and retention (Price et al, in press). To achieve their potential, students not only require appropriate facilities, knowledge, academic literacies, research and technical skills but also benefit from a supportive affective environment that supports dialogue, trust and self-efficacy. Consequently, ASKe is interested in finding ways to cultivate learning communities in which student involvement, participation and sense of belonging is increased, which will in turn improve the sharing of assessment expectations and standards and improve students' academic performance.

Here, we must introduce a note of caution and try to convey some clarity to the term 'community'. Lave and Wenger (1991: 98) describe community as a 'set of relations among persons, activity, and world'. Drawing from situated learning theory they conceptualise a community of practice as existing when newcomers move towards full membership and participation in the practices of a community, through mutual engagement, a sense of shared enterprise and a common repertoire of resources (including discourse). There are, however, inherent tensions in applying this organisational concept to academia, particularly around the role of students in academic communities. Which practice are students coming to know – that of the subject of their studies (such as accountancy or sports coaching) or that of studying itself? In this chapter we focus on assessment as the practice, and assessment is viewed in its broadest sense to include its multiple purposes beyond just that of judgement, with a particular focus on assessment as an act of learning in and of itself.

We should also acknowledge at this stage that strong communities have a downside. The more cohesive a sense of community the more exclusionary it may become. However, we see the positive potential of the community of practice (CoP) idea in providing a representational concept that challenges a transmission view of learning. Moving from a view of learning in which students are viewed and treated as passive recipients of the expertise of others, we approach a more democratic view in which students are enabled to assume a partnering role with their tutors in the learning process (O'Donovan et al, 2008).

Context

Supporting learning and improvement in students' academic performance is not an easy endeavour. However, arguably some contexts are more difficult than others. Although ASKe supports and contributes to assessment research and initiatives throughout the UK and internationally, the context for our community development is in the undergraduate programmes at the Oxford Brookes University (OBU) Business School. The OBU Business School is located on a satellite campus, a bus ride away from the hub of the university and unpublished local research has shown that the majority of students spend less than four hours on each visit to the campus. In addition, the undergraduate programmes are modular, with large class sizes particularly at Levels 4 and 5. Consequently, it has the potential to be an impersonal environment in which students could feel isolated from their tutors.

Cultivating community: reflections on our experience

While the CoP concept is established in higher education and many see CoPs as powerful environments for learning, there are few road maps for cultivating a true learning community that includes both students and staff.

Communities of practice are often recognised as separate from the formal structures and processes of the domains they inhabit, which suggests that too much control can hinder their evolution. However, Wenger et al (2002) suggest that a community's evolution can be 'shepherded' through the provision of structures, activities and opportunities that promote and support participation and give space and opportunity for enhanced interaction.

We focused on three main practical areas of activity (between which there is considerable interplay) while cultivating a community of assessment practice:

❏ The provision of 'affinity space' in which social learning can take place and the opportunity for informal and impromptu interactions enhanced.

❏ Increasing *intentional* opportunities for meaningful dialogue, interaction and collaboration both within and outside the formal classroom.

❏ Improving both staff and students' assessment literacy.

In getting started, one area of uncertainty and debate was and is the level of community that would be our focus. We all belong to multiple communities and as a baseline it was of interest to find out if students felt a sense of community or belonging to their institution, school or disciplinary programme. Early surveys replicated over two years elicited 488 responses from undergraduates at the end of their first year (Level 4). Findings from these surveys showed that only a minority of students (40%) felt a strong sense of belonging and this was to the institution, not to their department or programme. They attributed their affinity to interactions and relationships forged in their halls of residence and/or sports activities and student societies. The other 60% felt no or very little sense of belonging, attributing this to the lack of personal relationships with staff, large class sizes, living off campus and in the case of international students the difficulty in getting to know home students. These early baseline surveys showed that we had our work cut out. While a sense of belonging to the institution as a whole is to be valued, tacit knowledge of assessment, of learning expectations and of standards is held at programme or module level.

Affinity space

Our first step in developing community was the design and construction of 'affinity space' on our satellite campus. This was to support both social learning and informal and impromptu interaction between students themselves and with staff. The design of learning spaces is now acknowledged as having a powerful impact on student learning, engagement and assessed performance (Kuh et al, 2005).

The physical environment of Britain's oldest universities, Oxford and Cambridge, is built around the concept of community. A college system with central quadrangles and cloistered walks allowed largely monastic communities to live and work together in a relatively secure environment. Post-92 universities tend not to have been so lucky. Their legacy usually involves a mixed bag of functional spaces with few, if any, intentionally designed spaces to facilitate social learning and informal interaction.

Recently, however, funding of CETLs (Centres for Excellence in Teaching and Learning) has fuelled a growing interest in social learning space – spaces that combine social activities and learning activities with facilitative technology (Chism,

Figure 1 Café and entrance, the Simon Williams Undergraduate Centre, Oxford Brookes University

Figure 2 Celebrating the Chinese New Year

2006). ASKe has been no exception. After considerable research and visits to other such spaces in the UK, the centre's capital funding was used to design and construct a building, a social learning space, in the form of an undergraduate centre. A combination of café facilities, technology, flexible furnishings and support staff offices were designed to both support formal collaborative work and opportunities for informal interaction. Such a combination of facilities not only supports social learning, but also aligns with the integrated behaviours of the current generation of students.

When I was an undergraduate during the 1970s, assessment behaviours tended to be more individual and sequential. You researched and sourced information in a quiet library, subsequently typing up your research in a separate place while taking defined refreshment 'breaks'. These days, with wi-fi connectivity, our students research and collaborate on assignments in cafes, halls of residence and bars (9% of our 488 surveyed students declared that they frequently met in local pubs to do assessed group work). They favour places in which they can eat and drink, word-processing their work as they go – all the while in communication with others through email and mobile phones.

Within the first two years of the opening of the building at Brookes, a colonisation study was undertaken to both gauge colonisation behaviours and user preferences. Data collection involved online surveys, short surveys and 'mental mapping exercises' with students. Semi-structured interviews and focus groups were also undertaken with both staff and students and a group of undergraduate student researchers observed and surveyed building users four times daily for an academic year. It is clearly beyond this brief chapter to do justice to the final 60-plus-page internal report. However, headlines include:

❑ The importance of locating social learning spaces along main movement corridors of a campus to promote informal interaction.
❑ Ensuring connectivity with the rest of the campus environment through legible or recognisable connections with other spaces, both indoor and outdoor.
❑ Including natural light, flexible furniture and access to food and drink.
❑ Providing an internal layout that offers opportunities for both high visibility so students can see and be seen, but also places of refuge where students can tuck themselves away.

Prior research also suggests that spaces are more successful when they have a strong sense of identity. The interior decoration and ambience of the building was selected by students. A design firm put together a series of 'mood boards' depicting different interior decorative styles and large numbers of students voted for their preferred style over a period of a week. Interestingly, our undergraduates overwhelming voted for quite plain walls and flooring but with vivid, 'funky' furnishings, while postgraduate students and staff voted for a much more corporate style. The undergraduates got their way as it is, after all, a centre for undergraduates. If you visit, you may well be able to guess which the building is by the vivid colours of the furniture and movable screens when you look through the glass walls of the ground floor.

While the building has been robustly colonised by both staff and students, staff using the space for their own collaborative meetings and to socialise and eat and drink, the one disappointment has been that there is little informal interaction *between* staff and students. Students voice trepidation about approaching staff in the building. Arguably therefore, such physical affinity space is a necessary but not sufficient condition to cultivate a community that involves both staff and students. This finding emphasises the importance of *intentional* facilitation of formal and informal dialogue and interaction both face-to-face and online.

Enhancing formal and informal participation and dialogue

Like the layers of an onion, increased student participation can be facilitated at different levels in the assessment community. Here, the intention was to enhance student involvement and participation in:

❑ central, classroom-based assessment and feedback practices
❑ formal learning and assessment practices outside the classroom, and finally
❑ through opportunities to participate in informal activities outside the classroom.

Enhancing participation and engagement in formal classroom-based assessment and feedback practices

In the search for objectivity and reliability, traditional assessment practices often isolate and segregate the assessed from the assessors. Students write an essay, submit it and wait to hear back from an unknown reviewer to whom they are often anonymous. However, Rust et al. (2005: 231) advocate a 'social constructivist process model of assessment' in which students are actively engaged with every stage of the assessment process in order that they truly understand the complex and often tacit requirements of assessment. Following this model we seek enhanced student participation in assessment practice at three stages: pre-assessment, in the act of assessment itself and in feedback processes.

During the pre-assessment stage, prior research (Rust et al, 2003) has shown the effectiveness of engaging learners actively with assessment standards and criteria through a simple intervention in which they mark two exemplar assignments (one a bare pass and one an A grade), subsequently discussing and aligning their perspectives on the assignment qualities with each other and those of their tutors. Later, such 'trained' students can participate more fully in self-assessment or peer review and peer-assessment processes in which they can apply their knowledge of standards and criteria and become assessors themselves, improving their learning further from reading and reviewing the work of their peers and through peer dialogue. In some modules Level 5 and 6 students are asked to take part in assessment panels of Level 4 students' presentations. More recently, following current research (Price et al, in press), we are trialling across the school face-to-face feedback sessions in which individual or small groups of students engage in oral feedback dialogue with their tutors.

Active participation in even a relatively short, 90-minute, pre-assessment intervention has been shown to create a significant improvement in students' academic performance with an effect that lasts more than a year (Rust et al, 2003). That students should play a significant part in evaluative feedback of their own and others' learning, and be allowed to engage in dialogue about their learning with tutors, clearly constitutes a more participatory and less hierarchical assessment process and a departure from the traditional domination of the tutor role.

Enhancing participation in formal assessment and learning practices outside of the classroom

At the Business School we have run peer-assisted learning (PAL) for many years. Students who have successfully completed a module facilitate the learning of current students in optional sessions. PAL leaders are trained in facilitation techniques and published evaluation of the process (Price & Rust, 1999) demonstrates its effectiveness for both the leaders and participants. In this project we have extended such participatory roles to involve more students and to include a greater ability range.

One of the most successful new roles is that of 'module assistant'. Staff who lead modules with over 100 students (and there are many such modules in the Business School) have the opportunity to employ a student assistant. These students work in partnership with module leaders to organise the delivery of modules, engaging in many activities such as organising learning materials, monitoring attendance and analysing module evaluations. These partnerships achieve a range of useful outcomes. Students working in tandem with staff come to more fully understand the reasoning behind learning and assessment structures and processes. They become partners, jointly endeavouring to deliver worthwhile learning experiences. They engage in dialogue not just about the work at hand but also learning more about the other's experience of being a student or academic. This new understanding ripples out to their peers and colleagues to the benefit of all.

Another valuable role is involvement in pedagogic research. This includes students operating as research assistants, as in the colonisation study already described, but also involves students engaging in longitudinal research on the student learning experience. Students have the opportunity to become 'audio diarists' – they are given digital recorders to tape weekly commentary (about 10 to 15 minutes) on their student experience. Insights are wide-ranging and have helped us to come to know in more detail the lived experience of students, including, for example, assessment pressure points, students' thirst for a more personalised learning and the influence of outside pressures on their academic performance, such as when at the beginning of their second year (Level 5) many move into rented housing and deal with fraught house sharing and domestic issues, often for the first time. Other roles include that of technical assistant, facilitating other students' use of learning technologies, or assisting with undergraduate support services, manning coursework hand back services and, of course, the traditional roles of student ambassador and representative.

An unintended benefit is that we now have a significant number of engaged students who are willing and able to contribute in other ways. For example, the organisers of a recent pedagogic conference wanted a panel of undergraduate students to give a student perspective on the keynote (on stage and immediately after the presentation). Weeks of searching elicited no students prepared to do this, quite scary, task. Twenty-four hours and one email after we asked our students, we had a panel of five student volunteers confident that they could contribute. Participation fuels further participation.

Enhancing participation in informal activities outside the formal classroom

The final focus of our efforts to enhance student participation is through involvement with less formal, largely social activities. A 'carnival' reception is organised for new students in which they meet their personal tutors and are welcomed onto the campus to the smell of barbecue food, sounds of the samba and the vision of talented street performers (students and professionals). Programmes are encouraged and supported to organise staff and students events including Chinese New Year festivities, photography competitions and boat trips. Students themselves are encouraged to organise activities that bring students together. Funding is given to student groups who in a Level 4 module put together feasible event plans with the objective of building community, as well as academic credit at Level 5 if they elect to actually put the event

Figure 3 The Welcome Carnival, Oxford Brookes University Business School

on and reflect on the outcomes and experience. We also support student societies through a little seed money and help in negotiating university procedures.

Developing assessment literacy

The benefits of processes by which students develop self-evaluative abilities so that they can make informed judgements on their own work (and that of their peers) are not initially obvious to new students. New students tend to be absolute or dualistic in their understandings of the nature of knowledge and learning, believing in knowledge being certain, answers that are right and wrong and a clear divide between teacher and student. To the assessment-illiterate student the process of peer review can be viewed as just a way for tutors to shirk their marking responsibilities. An assessment-illiterate student is unlikely to make an effective PAL leader or student representative. Student evaluations drawn from assessment-illiterate, and indeed, pedagogically illiterate, students can be largely worthless. To take up a less authority-dependent role in their learning, students need to be able to make informed evaluations not only of their own learning, but also of their learning environment, including the teaching.

In the United States, formal pedagogic courses on learning have improved the quantity and quality of student contribution (Hutchings, 2005). However, many programmes have little room for a purpose-built course or module on pedagogy. Clearly, the participatory interventions already described in this chapter go some way towards orientating students into the assessment understandings and practices of a community. Marking practice, peer review and dialogic feedback practices build assessment literacy. However, arguably for real effectiveness they need to be intentionally and coherently developed. One lone peer-review experience is unlikely to build assessment literacy, indeed, it may by itself generate increased student resistance. A programme approach in which such interventions are sequentially and coherently developed by assessment literate staff is required. Arising out of the work of ASKe, students and staff have developed an 'assessment compact' (see website), now embedded in university policy, in which all university programmes are tasked with developing assessment literacy and co-ordinating assessment tasks across modules, not only to reduce assessment pressure points, but also for the coherent development of such understandings.

Lessons learned

This chapter has covered a lot of ground. When we consider making improvements to our assessment practice, we often focus on the development and evaluation of individual, focused, classroom-based initiatives. While these are to be applauded, the impact of such initiatives on the assessed performance of students will be greater when they are grounded in an intentionally designed learning environment in which student participation and involvement is sought and enhanced across a number of wide ranging activities. When such activities come together into an intentional and coherent orientation of students into a community of assessment practice, in which students' assessment literacy is developed along with affective dimensions, such as a sense of belonging and self-efficacy, the academic performance of students should dramatically improve.

Yet, while many of these individual interventions have been evaluated, and can be further examined by following references in this document and through visiting the ASKe website (http://www.brookes.ac.uk/ask), we have as yet, no definitive evidence on the holistic effect of these interventions. Perhaps, after only four years, could such evidence be realistically expected? This is a long-term project. We can point to many indicators of improvement, including student and staff perspectives and improvement of National Student Survey scores in some of our smaller, more coherent and personal undergraduate programmes. But definitive, holistic evidence remains out of reach. Improvements to learning are always difficult to quantify and attribute. Causality remains an issue. Sometimes in pedagogic research you have to rely on multiple 'straws in the wind'. The more straws bending in the same direction, the more conviction you can bring to your work.

References

Astin, A. W. (1993) *What matters in college: four critical years revisited*. San Francisco: Jossey-Bass

Chism, N. V. N. (2006) Challenging traditional assumptions and rethinking learning spaces. In Diana G. Oblinger (ed) *Learning Spaces*. USA: Educause

Hutchings, P. (2005) Building Pedagogical Intelligence, Carnegie Perspectives. Available online at http://www.carnegiefoundation.org/perspectives/ (accessed 27 May 2010)

Kuh, G. D., Kinzie, J., Schuh, J. H., Whitt, E. J. & associates (2005) *Student success in college: Creating conditions that matter*. San Francisco: Jossey-Bass

Lave, J. & Wenger, E. (1991) *Situated Learning. Legitimate peripheral participation*. Cambridge: Cambridge University Press

O'Donovan, B., Price, M. & Rust, C. (2004) Know what I mean? Enhancing student understanding of assessment standards and criteria. *Teaching in Higher Education* 9 (3) pp. 323–35

O'Donovan B., Price M. & Rust C. (2008) Developing student understanding of assessment standards. *Teaching in Higher Education* 13 (2) pp. 205–17

Price, M., Handley, K. & O'Donovan, B, (in press) Feedback all that effort, but what is the effect? *Assessment and Evaluation in Higher Education*

Price, M. and Rust, C. (1999) The experience of introducing a common criteria assessment grid across an academic department. *Quality in Higher Education* 5 (2) pp. 133–44

Rust, C., Price, M. & O'Donovan, B. (2003) Improving students learning by developing their understanding of assessment criteria and processes. *Assessment and Evaluation in Higher Education* 28 pp. 147–64

Rust, C., O'Donovan, B. & Price, M. (2005) A social constructivist assessment process model: how the research literature shows us this could be best practice. *Assessment and Evaluation in Higher Education* 30 pp. 231–40

Sadler, D. R. (2009) Indeterminacy in the use of preset criteria for assessment and grading. *Assessment and Evaluation in Higher Education* 34 (2) pp. 159–79

Wenger, E., McDermott, R. & Snyder, W. (2002) *Cultivating communities of practice*. Boston, MA: Harvard Business School Press

Yorke, M. (2002) Subject benchmarking and the assessment of student learning. *Quality Assurance in Education* 10 pp. 155–71

BERRY O'DONOVAN is a deputy director of ASKe, a Centre for Excellence in Teaching and Learning with a focus on sharing assessment standards (Assessment Standards Knowledge exchange). She is also the head of learning and teaching development in the Business School at Oxford Brookes University and a National Teaching Fellow. Berry primarily teaches on large, undergraduate modules with a focus on orientating new students into the academic demands of higher education. She has researched and published on assessment and feedback issues for over a decade.

2

'It made me think on my feet'
Encouraging non-written and part-written assessment

Jenny Anderson
Southampton Solent University

This chapter looks at a HEFCE-funded project in hospitality, leisure, sport and tourism designed to enhance the student learning experience by encouraging lecturers to develop inclusive modes of assessment which do not necessarily rely solely on the written word.

Introduction

Our project, called Towards Inclusive Assessment: Unleashing Creativity (it came to be known as the TLC project), aimed to encourage lecturers to review what and how they assess, rather than to advocate non-written and partly-written instead of written assessment.

Lecturers in focus groups were enthusiastic about more innovative forms of assessment. However, the challenge of time constraints and fear of student failure might have made them more risk-averse than they used to be. An audit of assessments on five courses in hospitality, leisure and sport, and tourism in three universities found 70% of all assessment was written. The Fund for the Development of Learning and Teaching (FDTL) financed this project to encourage lecturers to reflect on alternative forms of assessment which are less dependent on the written word during 2004–08 under FDTL Phase 5.

The intention was to empower lecturers to assess more innovatively. The project also urged lecturers to ask themselves whether written methods are the most appropriate way to assess learning outcomes and whether they best support the widening participation, employability and equality agendas of higher education. A website (www.creative.assessment.org) with case studies in oral, visual and practical assignments and underpinning research was set up.

The first objective was to develop and trial alternative forms of assessment and disseminate development resources highlighting the benefits of using partly written and alternative forms of inclusive assessment. The second objective was to develop the website to showcase existing practice and innovation in oral, visual and practical assessment areas and provide theoretical underpinning. Examples of assessments to be found on the web site include:

- ❑ Portfolio linked to placement
- ❑ Theatre role-play
- ❑ Dragon's den
- ❑ Setting up an exhibition
- ❑ Pitch and poster
- ❑ Market stall
- ❑ Multi-assessments for events
- ❑ Running an event
- ❑ Poster and exhibition
- ❑ Coaching and practical lesson plan
- ❑ Leaflet for target health groups
- ❑ Game show
- ❑ Role play viva for sport policy.

Rationale

As participation in higher education widens, we have more diverse learners with non-traditional entrance qualifications, varied backgrounds, unequal prior knowledge and experience and different learning styles (Brown and Glasner, 1999). Traditional assumptions about student background, study skills and conceptions of learning are no longer valid (Gibbs and Simpson, 2004). This growing diversity of the student population suggests that there is a need for more varied approaches to learning, teaching and assessment. As McCarthy and Hurst point out:

> all students have different learning styles, and it is still necessary to try to assess disabled students in a manner which best suits their learning style, rather than forcing students to fit into an 'accessible' mode of assessment (2001).

This implies that all students should have the opportunity to be assessed in ways that match their learning needs and preferences. So diversifying assessment methods would be instrumental in helping students meet learning outcomes and increase the likelihood that more students would experience opportunities for deep rather than surface learning.

Brown et al. suggest that student numbers, validation or moves to modularisation, greater diversity of students and greater understanding of 'graduateness' are reasons for lecturers to change the modes of assessment they offer to students. To this list of reasons might be added the growing number of vocational courses and more effective staff development, such as in-house lecturer training courses.

> It is fair to say that every assessment method will place some students at a disadvantage to a certain extent; it is our belief that we should adopt a range of assessment strategies so that students who are disadvantaged under one assessment method will have the opportunity to excel in others (1994: 50).

Context

The FDTL is supported by HEFCE (HEFCE 2003) and this fifth phase, building on the work of previous FDTL phases, aimed to

> reward and stimulate innovation and good practices in learning and teaching, and to disseminate such practices to secure the widest take-up among institutions. (HEFCE, 2003)

In Phase Five, starting in September 2004, £7m funding was available for projects at three levels, ranging from small-scale projects to large-scale projects (£250,000 over three years). The FDTL5 teams worked in partnership with Higher Education Academy senior advisers and subject centres.

The TLC project was based at Southampton Solent, Bournemouth and Oxford Brookes universities in the first year. Portsmouth, Leeds Metropolitan and Surrey universities were also involved in the second year. In the third year case studies were invited from all higher education institutions (HEIs).

Assessment, rather than teaching, influences student learning (Gibbs and Simpson, 2004) and improving the student learning experience is at the heart of higher education. Although there has been a shift in assessment practice from end-of-year examinations towards more continuous assessment and the acquisition and development of skills, standard written formats are still the basis of many assessments (McCarthy and Hurst, 2001). Assessment has often been based on a fairly narrow range of tasks, with (arguably) an emphasis on knowing rather than doing (Brown et al, 1994). The focus of much learning and assessment is written communication and for students who are dyslexic, for example, this can prove a continuous challenge, denying them the opportunity of fully demonstrating achievement of their learning outcomes.

Underpinning the argument for offering students a greater variety of assessment methods is the concept that students have different strengths. In the learning outcomes of a course, variety ensures that students all have a chance to be assessed in ways which are most appropriate to them and that they are better prepared for a range of skills and tasks in the workplace.

In a four-year Higher Education Academy survey 3,500 hospitality, leisure, sport and tourism final-year undergraduate students were asked about the best aspects of their courses (Chapman, 2005). The top three aspects identified by students were personal development (69%), variety and range of modules (53%), and learning academic skills (44%). Ranked eighth was 'mix of assessment methods'; for which there was a gradual decrease in satisfaction from 33% to 28% over the four-year period. The mix or variety of assessment types is increasingly seen as the most challenging and significant component of a student experience.

Research methodology

The primary research had three parts: an audit of assessment modes, lecturer focus groups and student in-depth interviews and focus groups. The lecturer and student focus groups and in-depth interviews were conducted using creative techniques not reliant on the written word.

An audit of assessment modes of five courses in hospitality, leisure, sport and tourism at three universities in the south of England was conducted covering 127 modules and 273 assessment modes. Data was analysed using SPSS (Statistical Package for Social Sciences). The method was based on an audit developed in the biological sciences field.

Focus groups were conducted with lecturers at the three universities in 2005 to explore their attitudes towards assessment. The aim of the focus groups was to evaluate staff experience of assessment, particularly non-written and partly written assessment, and to explore attitudes to change. Twenty lecturers teaching hospitality, leisure, sport and tourism attended three 90-minute focus groups. Lecturers had an average of 13 years teaching experience, with a range from two to 28 years. The average lecturer age was 45; there were 14 men and six women, of whom half had secondary, further and higher-education teaching qualifications.

Eighteen students attended two focus groups, and four students with dyslexia and one with a physical disability attended a separate focus group. The students were from all levels and from sport, leisure and tourism courses. The average age was 20; 65% were male and 35% female. They were all white and the majority were of British origin. In-depth interviews were conducted with students who participated in oral, visual and practical assessments at three southern universities. An experienced researcher who was not a lecturer conducted all the focus groups and interviews.

Results and evaluation

Assessment audit

An audit of assessment on five courses indicated that 70% of all assessments were written. The audit revealed a fairly traditional picture of essays, unseen examinations, reports and presentations. The amount of written assessment increased slightly from Level four to Level six on undergraduate degrees. Further analysis revealed that there were no significant differences with regard to module size (CATs), level, subject area and whether the module was core or option. However, at one of the three HEIs, module assessments were more likely to be written than at the other two. These findings were in line with the 2005 national survey of assessment practice in hospitality, leisure, sport or tourism in 49 HEIs and further education (FE) colleges (Chapman, 2005) where the same commonly used types of assessment were identified, but the order was slightly different (reports, essays, exams and presentations).

Lecturer focus groups

Lecturers were well aware of the links between learning, teaching and assessment and all were committed to improving the student experience. Lecturers talked enthusiastically about innovation and diversity in assessment. They had experienced working with a wide range of assessment types; the minimum number of types of assessments listed was 15 and the maximum number was 18.

Lecturers had mixed views on students' attitudes towards assessment. Some perceived students as being entirely assessment-driven and saw this as being detrimental to their learning. For example:

> A lot of our students are here for one purpose and that's to get a bit of paper rather than thinking of it in the bigger picture, of the broader learning and all the benefits that come with that.

Lecturers attributed this student view of an increasingly assessment-driven culture to a number of factors including the modular nature of courses, lecturers' protectiveness of their subjects and previous educational experiences.

> It's our [*the lecturers'*] fault. We've got into the culture where students only work when they have to do an assignment'.

Some staff were unhappy at students' approaches to learning, others felt that students were being realistic and learning the skills of time management which would set them in good stead for the future.

Lecturers and students can be suspicious of new assessment methods but, at the same time, both are aware of the shortcomings of traditional methods (McDowell and Sambell, 1999). Lecturers need to spend additional time reassuring students when they come across a new type of assessment for the first time.

Lecturers faced a number of challenges when making changes to module assessments; some of these were personal and others were institutional. The dominant themes were lack of time, fear of failure and lack of understanding about some theoretical aspects of assessment. Lecturers felt overwhelmed by the volume of work, particularly by marking and delivering good quality feedback in a reasonable timeframe.

At one institution lecturers led, on average, five modules. If each module had on average 2.3 modes of assessment, each lecturer would be responsible for setting approximately 12 assessments a year. This was felt to be challenging. It was also felt that it was difficult to be innovative when the number of students increases steadily. There were mixed views on whether sufficient resources were available to sustain the development and support of non-written assignments, which were seen as time-consuming to set up and maintain. The same was true for assessment which is individually negotiated between lecturers and their students.

Lecturers felt that an assessment-driven culture had led to their needing to set increasing amounts of work to ensure that students covered all the necessary materials in certain topics. Simply reducing the amount of work set was not the answer; they felt that they needed opportunities to give students ongoing feedback about their performance and assessments were the only way. Without extensive assessment, they feared that students would only cover limited amounts of their curriculum.

Fear of failure was mentioned by many lecturers and there were several variations on the theme. Some lecturers commented on their fears about external review, and professional and accreditation bodies, but at the top of the list was a fear of students failing. Retention is a cause for concern and there is growing awareness and disapproval of failing, or at-risk modules.

> I'm not particularly speaking for myself because I haven't tried to do this but you go through the processes, you set up an innovative piece of assessment – it goes wrong for some reason. You get quite a few students failing, you have an at-risk unit and you've got a failing unit where maybe you tried to do something different, and I think there is real fear and inertia because of that.

One experienced academic commenting on barriers to change at the TLC project steering group meeting said that what lecturers wanted most was to be liked by their students, and some lecturers had a fear that they might jeopardise this relationship.

With something as crucial as assessment, it is essential that innovation is not approached lightly, or engaged in for its own sake, because the consequences of getting it wrong are serious (Race, 1999). Rogers (1995) refers to this as 'triability' – the degree to which an innovation has been experimented on – the implication being that it is safer to run with something that has been tried and tested. It could be argued that lecturers are becoming more risk averse, and therefore may need more support if they wish to change the nature of their assessment (Anderson et al, 2006a). Interestingly, no one in the focus groups provided examples of innovative assessments which had failed.

Some lecturers expressed concerns about understanding elements of assessment theory and having an awareness of the benefits of different types of assessments. This is linked to limited experience and confidence in using alternative methods and also being able to refute charges of 'dumbing down'. Brown and Glasner (1999) noted that lecturers lacked awareness of alternative assessment methods, either identified through ignorance or fear about their use. They also felt that lecturers needed more technical awareness of how to make changes using university systems, how to write learning outcomes with the correct terminology and how to confidently write assessment criteria.

Validation, revalidation and periodic review were seen by some as a 'paper-exercise' and not an opportunity to review assessment methods. New modules are written as part of the validation or periodic review process. Ironically, this should be the time to reflect on learning, teaching and assessment but because lecturers frequently continue with their day job (teaching), the burden of extensive validation paperwork means some have even less time to reflect thoroughly on the assessment strategy.

Module-modification practice varies from institution to institution. Some HEIs have a twice-yearly opportunity to change assessment at module level and some are more rigid than others in the level of detail required. Assessment changes at one HEI had to be signed off by the department head, a minor-modification panel, and faculty board. Despite clear (but arduous) paperwork and plenty of notice given to lecturers, the signing off of the modification process came at one of the busiest times of the teaching year.

Elton and Johnson (2005) raise the question of how many innovations can be introduced before they fall foul of an institution's regulations. The implication is that fear about assessment changes are more perceived than real.

Student focus groups and in-depth interviews

Students were asked to reflect on various forms of assessment. They spoke about the important role of lecturers in either enhancing or undermining their learning experience. They spoke highly of practical forms of assessment, with examples including event management, presentations, coaching skills and video production. These forms of assessment were seen as positive for a number of reasons, including:

❑ Opportunities to put learning into practice
❑ Perceived relevance to future employment
❑ Development of skills
❑ Opportunities to fully express themselves which they felt some forms of written work did not always encourage
❑ Industry recognised qualifications
❑ Finished products they could take pride in
❑ Receiving immediate feedback.

Choice was valued because this increased motivation and independent thinking. Students generally said they disliked the pressure that examinations place on them and these were seen as negative and undermining experiences. Reasons included the time taken to revise, knowing how to structure their papers – 'it's getting it out of my head onto the paper', concentrating for the length of time needed and the weighting and consequently pressure on exam performance. Despite their profound dislike of exams, when asked whether they would get rid of them completely, most of them answered no. They felt that exams prove a basic competence in all areas, force them to study and showed they have 'earned' something by taking a degree. Instead, they argued for less weight on exams or replacing them with ongoing in-class assessment which allow them to revise smaller chunks and give them a better 'perspective' on their learning.

Students with dyslexia spoke in detail about the strategies they use to avoid taking subjects with examinations, even when they liked the subject area offered. They believe extra time brings its own challenges. They spoke about finding it difficult to concentrate for the additional time, being disturbed as other students leave the room and being stigmatised by having to remain in the room as other students leave.

Students referred to a range of non-written assessments and generally spoke very positively about them. Practicals, including coaching units and managing events, producing videos and presentations, were seen as encouraging assessment of a variety of skills relating to work in industry and supporting inclusivity. They also were seen as offering opportunities for personal choice and as enhancing individual confidence.

Group work was depicted as a mixed blessing. There is a general perception that students can end up carrying one another and that this makes the assessment 'unfair'. However, a number of the students commented upon the value of group work as it allows them to get real-world experience, develop self-awareness, exchange ideas and encourages students to get to know one another. Students don't necessarily welcome innovatory assessments and some may question motives behind the change of assessment, especially if it involves group, self and peer assessment (McDowell and Sambell, 1999).

Two key themes emerge from in-depth interviews with students: the stressful nature of oral and practical assessment and a lack of appreciation that formative assessment was intended to help prepare them for summative assessment.

Students' opinions about how assessment could be improved align remarkably well with currently available evidence (Biggs, 2003). They suggest:

❑ Encouraging ongoing learning with continuous assessment
❑ Setting clear criteria and hand-in dates
❑ Giving students time to prepare for their assessments
❑ Giving students the opportunity to choose the subject matter as this tends to increase their motivation and encourage independent thinking
❑ Listening to student feedback and then making changes to what you do.

How do non-written and part-written assessment help students learn?

Students valued and were motivated by choice in assessment and non-written and part-written assignments, which allowed them to put learning into practice and develop the skills they perceived to be relevant to future employment. Feedback indicates that students were motivated by different forms of assessment. Several referred to their enjoyment and the fact that they valued what they had achieved. Students involved in visual tasks commented that it helped them remember what they had been learning more effectively. Students involved in oral tasks felt they had to work harder to prepare but they could see the relevance of strong oral competency in later life. Students involved in complex and practical assessments reflected on the benefits to their soft skills and the fact that these experiences such as event management and coaching experiences would enhance their CVs.

By way of example, assessment in one unit moved from a traditional essay to a role-play viva to assess sport policy knowledge and understanding. An independent researcher ran individual and small-group in-depth student interviews with students after they had completed the assessment. Student feedback included:

❑ Stressful, however, powerfully rewarding
❑ A really good way of testing our knowledge and understanding of the subject – much more effective than presenting and writing
❑ It was an interesting change to the conventional assignments. It challenged me

more than a normal presentation or essay
❑ It was good, made me think on my feet.

Because this was a Level 6 unit and the lecturer was concerned about moving from an essay format, the percentage of oral assessment was gradually increased over a three-year period, allowing staff to become more experienced and confident in oral assessment at this level. The unit team who have run oral vivas for five years are now strong advocates of oral assessment and have been strongly supported by external examiners. Other forms of oral assessment are being trialled in different parts of the leisure and sport curriculum at this university.

Discussion

Students valued non-written and part-written assessment but they also found it stressful and found the group work a mixed blessing. The main rationale for offering a wide range of assessments is that students have different strengths, and variety in the learning outcomes of a course ensures that they all have a chance to be assessed in ways which are most appropriate to them and then they will be better prepared to face a wide range of tasks in the workplace.

While lecturers talked enthusiastically of innovation and diversity in assessment, the audit revealed a more traditional picture of essays, unseen examinations, reports and seminar presentations. Over two-thirds of assessment depends completely on the written word, although there are variations dependent on level and university.

If we assume that each student completes between 10 and 18 assessments in a year, the challenge is to create an assessment diet with an appropriate balance of different types of assessment. In HEIs with large modular programmes there are greater challenges in achieving this balance in assessment.

Lecturers were strongly committed to improving the student experience and understood the links between learning, teaching and assessment. It takes courage for a lecturer to step out of his or her comfort zone and introduce a completely new form of assessment. However, there are belt-and-braces approaches, such as involving external examiners in early discussions, trialling a new assessment method formatively and giving a new assessment mode a lower proportion of the total module marks.

There were a number of barriers which staff perceived as hindering change in assessment modes including lack of time and fear of student failure, which may be leading to a more risk-averse culture (Anderson et al, 2006b). There were differences between the three universities (Oxford Brookes, Solent and Bournemouth) in the study and over the three years of the study, changes in regulatory frameworks were taking place. At one university the focus on developing a more varied range of assessment with less dependence on the written word may have been a contributory factor in increasing the assessment and feedback National Student Survey scores each year for three years following the FDTL5 project.

Lessons learned

Since completing the three-year HEFCE funded project in 2008 there has been time to reflect on the research findings and the impact of running a pedagogic project on bringing about change.

- ❑ Early adopters and champions are essential in promoting assessment change because word of mouth is so powerful.
- ❑ The culture of individual workplaces should not be underestimated as a factor in encouraging or restricting change in assessment. Opportunities to raise awareness through staff-development activities and making accessible and meaningful resources available to staff are essential.
- ❑ The flexibility of regulatory frameworks for assessment change is an important factor.
- ❑ Well-funded projects can make a difference by raising awareness and encouraging a 'can do' atmosphere when supported by managers.
- ❑ Meaningful and accessible assignment exemplars with guidelines for those who are thinking about developing innovative assessment are useful. Fully worked exemplars are provided on the TLC website which for at least one university are linked to the learning and teaching website.
- ❑ It is challenging to understand why lecturers are motivated to make changes in their assessment and while many are keen to do so, there are considerable constraints. For those who want to bring about change in assessment recognising these constraints and finding ways of circumventing them is a priority.
- ❑ Measuring change in assessment modes is time consuming and cause and effect are hard to isolate in view of a fast changing HE environment.
- ❑ Following validation, there may be a low awareness of student assessment diet amongst lecturers teaching on those courses
- ❑ Reviewing the impact of assessment change is a slow process because the assessment cycle frequently takes a year.

How does this help students learn?

By providing a wider range of assessment opportunities throughout the curriculum students may be more motivated to learn because they perceive greater relevance to their future employment. While written skills are of great importance in the workplace students recognise that other skills such as oral communication and teamwork are of growing importance.

For some students, particularly those who are dyslexic, non- and part-written assessment provides a means to express themselves in different and potentially more satisfying ways. A wider range of assessment modes ensures that students have a great range of opportunities to put learning into practice, which again enhances their motivation.

References

Anderson, J., Jackson, C., Higgins, L., Bibbings, L. & Palmer, A. (2006a) Innovation in assessment: fact or fiction. In Wickens, Hose T, Humberstone B. (eds) *Current Trends and Developments in Pedagogy and Research*. Oxford: Oxford University Press

Anderson, J., Higgins, L., & Palmer, A. (2006b) Assessment: overcoming barriers to change. At Higher Education Academy annual conference 'Enhancing the Student Learning Experience' Nottingham.

Biggs, J. B. (2003) *Teaching for Quality Learning at University* 2nd edition. Buckingham: Open University Press/Society for Research in Higher Education

Brown, S., Rust, C. and Gibbs, G. (1994) *Strategies for diversifying assessment in higher education.* Oxford: The Oxford Centre for Staff Development

Brown, S. and Glasner, A. eds (1999) *Assessment Matters in Higher Education: Choosing and using diverse assessments.* Buckingham: SRHE

Chapman, T. (2005) *The student course experience survey 2005. A national Survey of final year students on hospitality, leisure, sport and tourism degrees.* Hospitality, Leisure, Sport and Tourism Network. Need web address

Elton, L. and Johnson, B. (2005) Changing assessment – danger of doing the wrong thing righter. At Student-Staff Partnership for Assessment Change and Evaluation (SPACE) conference, 9 November 2005, Plymouth

Gibbs, G. and Simpson, S. (2004) Conditions under which assessment supports students' learning. *Learning and Teaching in Higher Education* 1 pp. 3–31

Higher Education Funding Council for England (2003)

McCarthy, D and A. Hurst (2001) *A briefing on assessing disabled students.* Assessment series no 8. York: Learning and Teaching Support Network Generic Centre.

McDowell, L. and Sambell, K. (1999) The experience of innovative assessment student perspective. In S. Brown & A. Glasner (eds) *Assessment Matters in Higher Education. Choosing and Using Diverse Approaches.* Bury St Edmonds: St Edmundsbury Press

Race, P. (1999) Why Assess Creatively? In S. Brown & A Glasner *Assessment Matters in Higher Education. Choosing and Using Diverse Approaches.* Bury St Edmonds: St Edmundsbury Press

Rogers, E. M. (ed) (1995) *Diffusion of Innovations* 4th edition. New York: Freedom Press

PROFESSOR JENNY ANDERSON has taught for over 25 years in sport, leisure and tourism. Jenny has led over 20 industry consultancies in sport and outdoor recreation. In addition to assessment, her pedagogic research interests include lecturer induction and module leadership. She is dean of the Faculty of Business, Sport and Tourism at Southampton Solent University, and was director of the three-year £250,000 FDTL5 project about innovation assessment in hospitality, leisure, sport and tourism described in this chapter.

The author would like to thank members of the TLC project team for their contribution to the research and development that underpinned this paper: Lyn Bibbings, Oxford Brookes University; Liam Higgins, Southampton Solent University; Caroline Jackson, Bournemouth University; Alison Palmer, TLC Project Manager.

3

Assessing 'wicked competences' at a distance

Gabriel Reedy and Jill Mordaunt
The Open University Business School

How can higher education address some of the more difficult-to-teach and difficult-to-assess skills and competences – like collaborative work and research skills – especially at a distance? This chapter outlines and evaluates an assessment-driven approach and finds that new technologies can help to encourage deep learning about collaborative work and peer assessment.

Rationale and objectives

Both employers and the Quality Assurance Agency for higher education (QAA) require business studies degrees to prepare students for the world of work (QAA, 2007). Besides knowledge and understanding and critical engagement, however, there are softer skills that pose serious delivery challenges for all institutions. These skills, such as effective team working, on-line collaboration and giving and receiving feedback, are highly valued by employers and have been called 'wicked competences' (Knight and Page, 2007). They are also deemed to be difficult to assess.

As the team developing a new course *Business Organisations and Their Environments*, we wanted to take on this challenge and, by using new learning technologies, find ways of developing and assessing these competences in ways that would enhance students' employability. We were particular concerned to engage students in deep, meaningful learning about the relationship between business theory and their day-to-day practice. Rather than the more traditional notion of applying theory to practice, we hoped to encourage students to think of a more dialogic or reflexive relationship between the two.

At the same time, we needed to improve student retention. Students on long 60-CAT-point distance-learning courses often have a decline in motivation at around three to four months, and we thought that by introducing a completely different approach to studying at the course midpoint, we would help to re-motivate them and reinforce their learning. We therefore sought to develop an assessed activity for an assignment to fulfil a number of objectives:

❑ Engage the students in an on-line collaborative activity that would reflect and impact on their work practice.

❑ Increase retention by creating a new and exciting activity just when motivation is most likely to flag.

❑ Create an activity that has intrinsic worth for students.

Context

Even in face-to-face teaching environments, it can be hard to motivate students to undertake group work. Often this is deeply unpopular, particularly for highly motivated students who can resent being dependent on others for a really successful and highly marked assignment. In a distance learning setting like the Open University (OU) this can pose an even greater challenge. Convention has it that students choose the OU because of its flexibility. They usually have a much greater degree of freedom than full-time students about when and how they study. In contrast with conventional universities, OU students are generally experience-rich and time-poor. Thorpe (2009) reported the extent to which students juggle around tasks and often have to work in short concentrated bursts. However, the OU Business School student profile does resemble that of other higher education institutions (particularly post-1992 institutions) rather more than other OU student profiles.

In the cohort we evaluated, almost 25% of the students had English as a second (or third or fourth) language. 60% were under 30 – much younger and therefore more extrinsically oriented (i.e. motivated by the qualification, rather than intrinsically motivated by learning for its own sake) than the average slightly older OU student. Frequently, students study two or more courses at the same time (as well as working) to lessen the time on their journey to the degree. In this case, 38% were also studying at least one other course, often as well as holding a full-time job. However, the younger age profile does have advantages in that many of the students are both familiar with and comfortable with information communication technologies (ICT).

The other factor affecting OU students is geographical dispersal. Although the current offering of the degree is mainly in UK and Europe, in reality, OU students can be anywhere in the world. For example there are always a sizeable number in the armed forces who may have tour of duty in Iraq or Afghanistan. Tutorial attendance is optional and throughout the OU there has been trend towards students concentrating on electronic interaction via discussion forums and email, rather than attending face-to-face sessions, so the logistics of organising the activity can be complex. In these circumstances, introducing a requirement to work with others within a specified time-frame creates more challenges than students and their tutors usually have to manage.

As the university had very recently adopted a Moodle platform[1] as the basis for its virtual learning environment (VLE) and was adapting this for the OU context, the course team had the opportunity to use the collaborative tools to facilitate this learning. We were able to set up sub-groups on Moodle discussion forums for the

1 http://moodle.org/

students which enabled them to undertake the collaborative elements of the assignment online.

Description

Against this backdrop, the course team[2] decided first to look at other courses within the Open University for inspiration and experience. One member of the course team, for instance, had been involved with the design of an online scanning activity as a part of a postgraduate course in fundraising for non-profit organisations, and was convinced of the value of students gathering, assessing and using information from various sources. This sort of activity created a framework that could allow us to explore some of the other outcomes we wanted to achieve in the assessment, and so it became central to the assessment design.

The team's attention was also drawn to a short introductory course in health and social care, in which students were required to work together in small groups for an information-gathering exercise (Northedge, 2006). In this case, the highly structured software interface ensured student compliance with the process, and included elements for the formation of the groups, specific stage- and task-completion requirements, and an in-built discussion forum system enabling students to work together. The software also required students to complete their individual tasks before the group project was considered complete. One guiding principle behind the system was that it was 'fail-safe', so that students could not duck out of their participation in the process (Northedge, 2006).

The benefits of Northedge's system were not just superficial and were reflected in both the student and tutor feedback on the course. Students were freed from the organisational burdens of group work, considered especially onerous in distance- and blended environments, and they could focus on the tasks at hand. The tasks themselves were quite clearly structured, leaving little room for ambiguity or confusion. Finally, the system imposed on each student the burden of completing his or her personal tasks (with a clear visual marker, seen by all students in the group, as to each fellow student's status) so that the group project could be completed.

As we considered the design of the collaborative assignment for the course, the course team began to wrestle with some of these and other pedagogical issues. After all, group work in the real world of business is rarely a simple and structured experience with clearly laid-out tasks and an in-built, at-a-glance management system. How could some of the benefits of the web-based group activity be achieved without the highly structured software interface? Were there ways that students could be encouraged – by the design of the assessment – to participate in the activity? Could

---

2   At the Open University, the course team is made up predominantly of permanent members of academic and academic-related staff who design, write, and produce a course module. Associate lecturers, or tutors, are part-time academic staff who teach the course around the regions and nations of the UK, as well as internationally

we design the assessment so that it felt to students like a genuine learning experience, rather than another assessment burden? And finally, could we do all of these while meeting the learning outcomes we wanted to achieve?

The course team felt that, while it was a considerable challenge, these and other issues could be dealt with in the assessment project. The design of the assessment activity began to take shape with a number of key features:

- ❏ **Assessment can be authentic**
  From one perspective, assessment is a necessary evil that is often designed for the benefit of teachers and examiners. However, it can also be a learning experience in which students have a chance to try new ways of thinking and working in a low-risk environment. It can also be designed with elements that reflect the 'real world' of the discipline or field of study.

- ❏ **Student choice**
  Students have both the choice of the focus for their assignment, and also work together to negotiate the criteria for evaluating what they find in their search.

- ❏ **Assessment of, and through, the process**
  The assessment design focuses not only on what the students produce, but how they engage in the process. The outputs are only part of the activity. Marks are awarded for participation in the process as well as the final product, so that students cannot attempt to produce a passing piece of work while opting out of the process.

- ❏ **Peer review**
  The process attempts to help create and foster a sense among students that they can learn from each other rather than just from their tutor and their course material. By designing a process that pushes students to each other for their first feedback experience – and by asking structured feedback of them for their student colleagues – the activity builds an ethos of collaborative knowledge creation. Importantly, peer review gives students not just a chance to learn about their own work, but to learn from what they see in others' work as well.

- ❏ **Conducting, and evaluating the products of, online research**
  Students' first port of call for research is often the Internet and other online resources, yet frequently this research is not directed and the results are not clearly evaluated. The process pushes students to triangulate their information sources.

- ❏ **Scaffolding the learning, even in an assessment activity**
  At each stage of the process, students need to be supported in their work. These supports can be fairly minor – perhaps only an explanation of what is expected – but are nonetheless crucial to the learning process. Sometimes that scaffolding can be field- and discipline-specific, such as referring to sources of authority in a field.

❑ Making learning techniques explicit helps students learn

Meta-cognitive approaches explicitly point out what is happening in a learning setting to students, so that they begin to learn how to learn and why learning in particular ways is beneficial. These can make a positive difference for student learning. For example, often students don't understand the point, the process, or the value in peer review. Outlining and explaining these things gives students the chance to participate actively in the process and understand what is expected.

❑ Individual and collaborative work are both important

Individual production of academic work, the mainstay of traditional assessment activities, is valuable and important. But collaborative processes can improve the quality and the learning experience associated with that individual work.

❑ Managing group processes

In the real world of work, people often have to come together to work with people to accomplish a shared and common goal. Occasionally, these groups have problems with interaction or execution. In this process, students are faced with that reality and encouraged to work through any problems that arise.

❑ Staged design

Because the process is such a valuable part of the learning experience, each stage of the assessment feeds into the next. Rather than attaching small amounts of marks to each step, the design of the process encourages students to go through each step. In order to complete the activity in the second stage, a student needs the inputs that are products of the first stage.

The completed assessment consists of four basic stages, and each corresponds to 12–14 hours of work for students. During the first stage of the exercise, students have two basic tasks to accomplish. They are asked to choose a field of work, an organisation or a particular job role that they aspire to and to begin online research into what working in that area might be like. While that research is ongoing, students begin to work together to come up with their own agreed group list of criteria for how they might judge and assess the evidence they have collected. Students are given a prompt to begin to work from, in the form of the results of a survey from the Chartered Institute of Management.

Continuing that negotiation process into the second week of the activity, they finalise their list of criteria, and their chosen research focus, and begin writing their individual report. In the third week of work, they finish their individual report and post it for their peers to review. Finally, in the last week, each student reviews the work of two colleagues, providing structured and focused feedback based on the learning outcomes of the activity, while receiving feedback from two colleagues on their own work. Using that feedback, students have the opportunity to rewrite and augment their work to take into account what they have learned. To reinforce the value of the peer review process, students are asked to write a small reflective paragraph on the feedback process explaining their perspectives on, and use of, the feedback they received (see Figures 1 and 2 below).

Evaluation

The course team was committed to closely monitoring the first year delivery of the course in order to evaluate the reception and the outcomes of the assessment; this

---

Learning outcomes

Because these weeks are focused on completing the fourth assignment of the course, the learning outcomes for these weeks are slightly different than in other weeks. To complete these weeks' work, and in submitting your assignment, you will demonstrate your:

¶ ability to research issues concerning domestic and international business organisations and their environments
¶ critical thinking, analysis and synthesis
¶ ability to evaluate and compare competing perspectives
¶ critical appraisal of a range of materials drawn from a variety of sources and selection of the salient issues and arguments from these
¶ effective communication of information, arguments and ideas using language and styles appropriate for a business context and audience
¶ ability to work effectively in a team environment in a virtual context
¶ effective self-management of time, good planning, individual initiative and enterprise.
¶ use of interpersonal skills appropriate to business such as negotiation, persuasion and presentation
¶ application of course ideas to your own interactions with organisations and your own life experiences.

Figure 1 Excerpt from course website

Listen to this page | Accessibility | Gabriel Reedy (01985221) | StudentHome | TutorHome | IntranetHome | ─o Sign out | Contact us

The Open University | Study at the OU | About the OU | Research at the OU | Search the OU

B201-09B > Group collaborative activity ... > Structure of Weeks 17-20   (Search this document)

◀ Previous: **Learning outcomes for Weeks 17-20**

Structure of Weeks 17-20

Week 17 TMA 04: Selecting an area of work

In the first week of the exercise, you will choose a field of work to explore and begin to research what it might be like to work in that field, including in a particular organisation or job role. In collaboration with your colleagues, you will begin to develop your own list of criteria of what you think is important in a workplace or a career.

Week 18 TMA 04: Choosing your organisation

In the second week of the exercise, you will finalise your list of criteria with your colleagues. You will pick one of the organisations you identified in the previous week and use it as the focus of the rest of the exercise. You will research information on the employer and the sector you've chosen, and begin planning and writing your report.

Week 19 TMA 04: Sharing your preliminary report

You will finish writing a report of approximately 1000 words and share it with two of your colleagues for feedback. You will read two of your colleagues' reports and provide structured feedback on their work.

Week 20 TMA 04: Giving feedback and submitting your TMA

Using the feedback you received from your colleagues, you will make any changes or additions to your report. Your TMA submission will include your original report, the feedback you received from your colleagues, and your rewrite that incorporates the feedback you received.

Next: **Resources for Weeks 17-20** ▶

OU on TV | For Alumni | For Employers | Privacy | Conditions of Use | Copyright | Cymraeg | Jobs | News | Donate
© The Open University +44 (0)845 300 60 90 Email us

Figure 2 Structure of the assessment with week-by-week activity descriptions

was achieved using a variety of approaches. Because the course was based on the university's Moodle-based virtual learning environment, an asynchronous conferencing system was, from the start of the course, open to both course tutors and members of the course team. In attempting to create an environment of support and responsiveness to tutor concerns, the course team actively encouraged tutors to direct feedback, questions, issues and concerns to this forum. Because this assessment occurred some four months into the course, tutors were quite comfortable using the forum, and posted to it frequently.

During the first presentation of the course, many of the early forum postings were concerned with the specifics of the assignment – tutors enquiring of their colleagues about advice to give to students, checking in to make sure that the process went smoothly and querying the technical details about how marks would be awarded. But there were also some quite clear anxieties about the tutor role in such an unusual assessment. There was also anxiety about whether students would 'do' the collaborative work, or whether the group interaction would actually happen. The online community, however, helped mitigate some tutors' concerns. Like several of his colleagues, one tutor posted how pleased he was about how his groups were getting on with the work without much input from him; 'I think,' he wrote, 'that some of the real learning for them lies in them doing that.'

Once the deadline for student submission had passed, the tone of the postings changed, as tutors began to mark the assignments. Because the process generated a fairly large amount of material – postings to the small-group discussion forums, the individual reports, and students' peer reviews of each others' work – tutors found this assignment much more time-intensive to mark than previous traditional-style assessments. The forums also began to fill with tutors reporting their students' feedback, usually unsolicited, on the process, which was mostly overwhelmingly positive.

Students talked about how it helped them re-evaluate their professional and career goals and how it gave them a new perspective on what tutors go through in marking student work. One student mentioned that, of over 25 assignments for Open University courses he had completed, this was the most enjoyable assessment experience he had had. Another talked about the assessment as one of the 'most constructive academic activities I have ever done', partly because of the innovative approach to group activity. Many students talked about the peer review process as being a powerful learning experience, citing the challenges of learning to give useful feedback and of taking into consideration their peers' comments on their own work.

Interestingly, some students framed any frustrations they might have had with the assignment in terms of learning experiences. Instead of venting their frustration about the asynchronous nature of the forums, one student talked about how the lack of ability to fall back on face-to-face contact in a collaborative setting showed how careful and attentive one had to be to the online activity.

Further evaluation included the quality-assurance process of monitoring tutor marking; a process that echoed some of the trends initially spotted in the tutor forums. Monitors reported that students seemed to be giving cogent and focused feedback, and that their comments often made reference to the learning outcomes of the project or to specific course themes and theories. Further evaluation of the process, based on an analysis of students' interaction with the process and their feedback to colleagues, is currently underway.

Conclusion

Overall, the outcomes of the first presentation of the course indicate that it is possible to design and deliver an assessment that addresses some of the so-called 'wicked' competences that are so often avoided in formal assessments in higher education, while also creating a learning experience that students find relevant and enjoyable. Further, it is possible to encourage students to collaborate on assessment activities without undue fear that doing so will compromise the integrity of the assessment. Finally, these tasks can be accomplished even when working in blended and distance-learning environments.

References

Knight, P. and Page, A. (2007) *The assessment of 'wicked' competences – Report to the Practice-based Professional Learning Centre.* The Open University, Milton Keynes http://kn.open.ac.uk/public/document.cfm?docid=8933

Northedge, A. (2006) 'Designing a fail-safe online group project work environment'. In *e-Learning: Learning Theories vs. Technologies?* Bangkok, Thailand, Ramkhamhaeng University

QAA (2007) *Subject Benchmark Statement: General business and management.* The Quality Assurance Agency for Higher Education Gloucester. At http://www.qaa.ac.uk/academicinfrastructure/benchmark/statements/GeneralBusinessManagement.asp

Thorpe, M. (2009) *Learners' Experience of eLearning in Practice Course. Overview of the Student Case Studies.* The Open University, Milton Keynes http://kn.open.ac.uk/document.cfm?docid=12151

JILL MORDAUNT is a senior lecturer in social enterprise and is head of department in the Public Leadership and Social Enterprise Centre. She joined The Open University Business School in 1994 as director of the Voluntary Sector Management Programme. She and her team were recently awarded an Open University teaching award for her work on developing innovative approaches to learning using new technologies.

GABRIEL REEDY is a lecturer in higher education at King's College, London, and was a curriculum innovation fellow and lecturer in teaching and learning innovation at the Open University from 2006 until 2009. He is also an associate lecturer with the Open University. His research interests focus on how technology can enhance learning environments and support innovative pedagogies.

4

Closing the loop
Tutor engagement in formative assessment for an impact on the learner experience

Stylianos Hatzipanagos
King's Learning Institute, King's College London

How much can assessment activities be used to enhance dialogue, interaction and collaborative work and consequently improve learning, and how are these activities perceived by tutors and students? This chapter looks at tutor and student perceptions of how assessment activities improve learning.

Introduction

The chapter reports on two projects exploring tutors' and students' perceptions of assessment to establish how far assessment activities are used to enhance dialogue, interaction and collaborative work and consequently improve learning, and how these activities are perceived by tutors and students. Data was collected from three open and distance learning (ODL) environments – King's College London, the external programmes of the University of London and the Open University (OU). This chapter presents a conceptual model of formative assessment and discusses how this can be made to work purposefully to support students in higher education.

The objectives of the investigation were to:

❑ Put forward a conceptual model of formative assessment based on the literature and explore whether this model has any implications for learning and teaching in 'real' environments.

❑ Promote an understanding of the significance of formative assessment by establishing and comparing attitudes to assessment amongst tutors and students.

❑ Identify current feedback practices and examine whether these practices support formative assessment and identify examples of good practice of formative assessment.

It was hoped that the projects would benefit assessment stakeholders in higher education, in particular tutors, students and policy makers. Participating tutors were encouraged to reflect on assessment practices and support mechanisms and tools that are required for effective formative assessment. These tutors were distance-learning tutors from a range of disciplines in the three participating institutions. A significant part of their role was to mark and comment on student work. Undergraduate and postgraduate students could benefit by engaging in dialogue in relation to feedback and participating in innovative assessment activities, such as peer- and self-assessment. In addition, the outcomes could have an impact on policy by informing practice about different types of assessment and the use of more interactive feedback.

Rationale

In a face-to-face context, higher education institutions (particularly research-led ones) have sometimes been concerned more with examining than learning and teaching. This has led to an emphasis on summative assessment, or assessment for accreditation. By contrast, open and distance learning (ODL) environments have tended to emphasize the necessity of formative assessment practices. Distance education in general has been proactive in developing innovative formative assessment, out of a need to find ways to provide systematic feedback to students in the absence of direct contact and interaction with tutors in a campus setting. Assessment methods in distance learning contexts can benefit from an element of dialogue. Different disciplines and learning environments (campus-based or distance learning) use different approaches to assessment, and comparison of approaches can lead to a cross-fertilisation of good practice across disciplines/institutions.

These projects focused on formative assessment, that is assessment which yields information useful for tutors and students 'to modify the teaching and learning activities in which they are engaged' (Black & Wiliam, 1998a: 2). Juwah et al. (2004) have developed a model of formative assessment that offers a synthesis of current thinking by key researchers in this area, including Sadler (1983, 1989), Black and Wiliam (1998b), Torrence and Pryor (1998) and Yorke (2003).

Among the seven key principles of formative assessment identified by Juwah et al, is the encouragement of dialogue around learning as fundamental to effective feedback practices. In this discourse, the learner is at the centre of the model and an active participant in monitoring his/her performance and in closing what has been termed the loop (Sadler, 1989). In this study, the understanding of feedback as dialogue was fundamental to the process of 'closing the loop'.

Communication forms part of the mechanism by which the learner monitors, identifies and then is able to 'bridge' the gap between current learning achievements and the goals set by the tutor. This view of feedback as an active, participative process, contrasts with the notion of feedback as a transmission process that involves 'telling' or passing on information. In other words, communication becomes a vital part of the feedback cycle that enables students to actively construct their own understanding of what can be complex and difficult messages to decipher (Higgins et al, 2001). Nevertheless, to be formative, the feedback should involve some level of dialogue amongst both the students and between the tutor and the student. This dialogue should result in negotiated points of action and monitoring of progress by the tutor, which has not been always the case in our data (Hatzipanagos and Warburton, 2009).

Learners are the object of assessment, reacting to an imposed process, and tutors are the dominant group: adult learners should have a role in the assessment process (Leach et al, 2001). This notion of feedback as dialogue probably 'disempowers' the tutor by redressing the balance of power, but it can be seen to empower the student. The outcome/product of this dialogue can be disconcerting for the students as there is no 'pre-determined' handed-down set of judgements, but a mutually constructed set of targets that the students will act upon.

Adopting a view of feedback as dialogue and student empowerment leads to an emphasis on assessment strategies that involve the learner at various stages: participating in the assessment setting process, which may include different types of involvement (for example, peer- and self-assessment, negotiating assessment criteria, constructing assessment questions). Peer or self-assessment and collaborative learning can enhance dialogue and increase the formative aspects of student learning.

e-Assessment has certainly enriched conventional assessment methods (Whitelock, 2009). New technologies provide an opportunity for using different types of assessment and expanding the range of formative practices of assessment. Computer-mediated communication is the essential medium that underlies e-assessment to support feedback. The provision of feedback is enhanced by the interactive, timely and continuous qualities of the medium.

Context

This project explored a range of formative assessment practices and examined how they are implemented in ODL environments in higher education. It identified tutors' perceptions and attitudes towards assessment and investigated the relationship between formative assessment and learning technologies in the light of the potential these technologies offer.

Following semi-structured interviews with tutors focusing on their perceptions of assessment and evidence of dialogue and interaction around formative assessment and feedback, the collected evidence contributed to identifying individual cases of practitioners employing formative assessment. It explored assessment practices in distance education with a focus on tutors' orientations. The concept of orientation used in this research was used to describe a pattern of beliefs that stems from tutors' assessment practices and their explanations of those practices (based on Samuelowicz & Bain, 2002).

The aim was to encourage the cross-fertilisation of assessment practices between different learning environments, where summative assessment sometimes dominates. Of the three environments, the King's College ODL and the external programmes were broadly similar, and there were also consistent elements of good practice. As far as the external programmes are concerned, there was evidence of huge variety of practice. This was to be expected in a diverse system across the spectrum of disciplines, institutions and target audiences that constitute the external system of the University of London. In contrast, the OU has the infrastructure to provide systematic provision of feedback; in addition, they have a framework which emphasises periodic assessment rather than end of year assessments.

Twenty tutors and 17 students from the three ODL environments participated in open-ended interviews. We aimed to include tutors and students from the same disciplines. Where that was not possible we looked at courses which had a similar disciplinary context, so the context would not be dissimilar. Samuelowitz and Bain's (2002) differentiation of learning-centred and teaching-centred disciplines allowed us to encounter a broad classification of disciplines. An online questionnaire based on the interview outcomes was administered to a large cohort of students and in the three environments; there were 1,032 returns.

Description

Analysis of the data revealed that institutional cultures and the nature of an institution determine what assessment practices are used and how they are implemented. The outcomes can be summarised in four major categories:

Impact of policy on tutors' practice

We examined the current policies, guidelines and documentation in relation to the provision of formative assessment and feedback at both local and institutional levels. We looked for evidence of formative assessment practices in institutional documents such as institutional and departmental learning and teaching strategies, handbooks of assessment and course approval forms. The idea was to investigate the existence of explicit/implicit guidelines on feedback provision. However, while most of the documents seemed to encourage innovation and diversity in summative assessment methods, in order to ensure the best possible opportunities for student learning or for the course leaders/tutors' benefit, they did not make a clear distinction between summative and formative assessment practices.

Tutor engagement

Despite the frequent occurrence of assessment guidelines for practitioners, there is sometimes a disjunction between beliefs, ambitions and pragmatic approaches to the use of formative assessment. Analysis of the data revealed that the practitioners' attitudes to formative assessment depended on the context in which they operated, and were discipline-oriented. The first classification of approaches in the project was in two substantial groups and one smaller group. The first two held tutors who claimed that they were proponents of formative assessment: they either used formative assessment in their practices (group 1) or claimed that they did not; however they would consider it if pragmatic constraints allowed (group 2). The third smaller group held those that did not consider formative assessment necessary in their context.

A significant number of tutors in our study recognised and valued the formative aspect of summative assessment. According to their responses, the assessment policies determined but did not constrain the methods of assessment they used. However, a smaller number of tutors felt constrained by the policies on assessment and the particular assessment set-ups, and this determined their decision not to innovate. For these, the feedback provided was generally seen as predetermined by the types of assessment used and did not appear to have a formative role.

The range of assessment methods available included:

❑ essays, assignments and exams
❑ multiple-choice questions
❑ objective structured clinical examinations (OSCEs) in a clinical setting
❑ assessed contributions to online tutorials
❑ word-processed assignments submitted online
❑ portfolios
❑ mock exams
❑ project reports
❑ research proposals
❑ social software outputs, such as in blogs and wikis.

From the methods of assessment used, those that included an element of dialogue were considered the most formative. Overall, the notion of 'formative' varied; for example, often it was equated to 'continuous assessment'. In courses where exams were the primary method of assessment, no feedback was provided with the exception of courses where some feedback could be given upon request. Peer- and self-assessment and collaborative learning were seen by the tutors as the most formative practices, but interestingly they were not used extensively.

Student engagement

The findings suggested that the target audience of institutional groups of students had diverse perceptions of assessment. Analysis of the data revealed that students' attitudes to assessment were not discipline dependent. It was the broad context (the ODL environment) that determined attitudes. They were overall positive to the use of e-assessment; however, the majority recognised the challenges in providing a suitably formative environment in these settings.

Students had some difficulty in defining their personalised learning environment and the 'affordances', that is, the intended, prescribed functions of the technology, but also the unintended consequences of the learning technology tools they used (Conole & Dyke, 2004). For instance, some of the students showed very little appreciation of true/false computer based quizzes as tools for engaging learners, and described them as 'superficial'. Others thought that electronic annotation of an assignment by the tutor allowed better integration of the feedback into the assessment process, further facilitating dialogue.

Formative e-assessment

The projects considered whether current formative assessment practices can benefit from learning technologies and the opportunities for participation and dialogue in the rise of emerging learning technologies, using tools such as social software and electronic portfolios. These included all those practices that promote and support student dialogue.

As a result, it was necessary to set a weighting against certain methods of assessment. We rated as low those assessments that do not facilitate dialogue, e.g. end-of year assessments are usually problematic in this respect, for objective reasons – the students do not have the opportunity to engage in feedback cycles – and consequently the 'closing the loop' cycle cannot be completed. Whereas methods of assessment that generate dialogue between tutor and students about the assessment outcomes, with agreed action points and monitoring of progress, have a strongly formative nature.

Tutors used a range of technologies that can support learning, although they are not clearly formative in nature, for example:

❑ Objective tests, though they 'disagree' with certain disciplines, particularly in humanities, where tutors saw them as irrelevant to the 'discursive' quality that student answers should have.

❑ Model answers, received or revealed after students submitted their answer, as non-personalised feedback.

❑ Electronic submission of assignments or projects, as this is perceived to encourage more comprehensive provision of feedback.

❑ e-Assessment technologies that had a strong formative nature and were used to assess different aspects of student learning were:

➲ Communication tools in virtual learning environments

➲ Online tutorials where contribution/quality of contribution was linked to assessment

➲ Games that allowed monitoring and intervention

➲ Audio, to canvas opinions/understanding of concepts/issues, where audio was perceived to be more conceptually meaningful than video

➲ Custom-made tools such as certainty-based marking to improve the impact/ function of multiple-choice questions

➲ e-Portfolios as reflective tools

➲ Videoconferencing

➲ Social software tools, especially blogs and wikis.

An evaluation framework was used to assess progress against the set objectives. An evaluative mid-term report addressed issues such as assessment policies, results of the pilot study and the development of a formative assessment framework. A post-questionnaire was used to provide opportunities for feedback from the participants and assessed changes in their attitudes towards formative assessment and feedback, and evaluated effectiveness of resources produced by the projects.

Discussion

The implication is that a categorisation of assessment practices in four stages (Table 1) could benefit tutors working in different disciplines by encouraging them to move from stage zero (limited evidence of engagement with formative assessment practices) to stage three (making formative assessment central in teaching practices).

Table 1   Embedding formative assessment practices in the assessment cycle

Stages	
Stage zero	❏ Assessment mostly through exams and end of assessment term projects. ❏ No provision of feedback. ❏ Limited or no peer/self-assessment opportunities. ❏ Limited or no use of learning technologies to support assessment practices.
Stage one	❏ Generalised feedback on student work with limited customisation to the needs of the individual learner. ❏ Examiner reports with model answers for monitoring/evaluating assessment practice. ❏ Use of learning technologies to support assessment through objective tests
Stage two	All the above in stage one plus: ❏ Periodic/continuous assessment for learners to rehearse arguments that they will use in end of assessment period assessments. ❏ Feedback is monitored, to ensure that students will act upon negotiated targets and the feedback loop is closed. ❏ Learner responses to feedback become an essential part of the assessment cycle. ❏ Use of learning technologies such as computer mediated communication to facilitate the assessment cycle.
Stage three	All the above in stage two plus: ❏ Peer/self-assessment. ❏ Student involvement in setting marking criteria. ❏ Use of learning technologies to peer-review and to construct knowledge collaboratively.

Stage zero

In stage zero assessment is implemented mainly through exams and end-of-assessment-term projects. In this set up, feedback on performance is either limited or non-existent. There are no opportunities for peer/self-assessment and there is no use of learning technologies to support assessment practices.

Exams are a common assessment method in higher education. However, in 'end-loaded' assessments such as end-of-year exams, students do not benefit from feedback. Implementation of formative assessment practices and the provision of feedback can be problematic in courses where the emphasis is on end-of-year assessments, as the 'closing the loop' component of the assessment process very rarely takes place.

Stage one

Stage one is characterised by the provision of generalised feedback on student work. By default, this is of limited customisation to the needs of the individual learner. There is limited use of learning technologies to support assessment practices.

A drawback in providing generalised feedback is that it is not tailored to the needs of individual students, unless the tutor has customised it. A more adaptive approach tailored to learner needs would benefit the students. This can be logistically difficult with big cohorts of students. However, a solution could be a concise template including feedback on performance and developmental issues which the students would need to consider. This template (very close to a generic feedback sheet) could be adapted/personalised quite easily by the tutor for every student.

Examiner reports with model answers are also used to monitor and evaluate assessment practice. Examiners' reports for the use of tutors and students are useful because they are not model answers to exam questions but a concise and sometimes reflective account of the issues, related to a correct approach to answering assessment questions.

Stage two

Periodic/continuous assessment is central in stage two, helping learners to rehearse arguments that they will use in end of the assessment period assignments. The notion of continuous assessment now established in some distance learning institutions tends to be periodic rather than continuous in nature. Some form of periodic assessment is necessary to ensure that monitoring progress and study-support measures are available to the students before they reach the final assessment. However, even periodic assessment can play a summative role, where students are not given an opportunity to revisit and use the feedback subsequently.

Feedback is monitored, using computer mediated communication, to ensure that students will act upon negotiated targets and the feedback loop is closed. In this way, learner responses to feedback become an essential part of the assessment cycle.

Stage three

Peer- and self-assessment play an important role in stage three, as do activities designed to help students to acquire ownership of the assessment process. These may also take the form of student involvement in setting marking criteria.

Use of learning technologies to peer-review and to construct knowledge can facilitate assessment activities. Further emphasis on formative assessment can be facilitated by the use of computer communication tools that encourage dialogue about feedback and assessment (such as blogs and wikis, synchronous and asynchronous discussion forums and social networking tools).

Conclusion

In this research, we considered feedback, intertwined with the notion of dialogue, as a two-way communication between the student and the tutor and also among the students themselves. Our evidence suggests that assessment and e-assessment practices which involved the provision of formative feedback seemed to encourage student self-assessment and self-regulation.

The projects contributed to the development of a framework for rationalising formative assessment practices. In this framework, assessment methods are most effective if they move practitioners and students towards the use of formative assessment.

References and URLs

Black, P. & Wiliam, D. (1998a) Inside the black box: Raising standards through classroom assessment. *Phi Delta Kappan* **80** (2) pp. 139–48

Black, P. & Wiliam, D. (1998b) Assessment and Classroom Learning. *Assessment in Education: Principles, Policy and Practice* **5** (1) pp. 7–73

Conole, G. & Dyke, M. (2004) Understanding and Using Technological Affordances: A Response to Boyle and Cook. *ALT-J* **12** (3) 301–317

Hatzipanagos, S. and Warburton, S. (2009) Feedback as Dialogue: Exploring the Links between Formative Assessment and Social Software in Distance Learning. *Learning, Media and Technology* **34** (1) pp. 45–59

Higgins, R., Hartley, P. and Skelton, A. (2001) Getting the message across: the problem of communicating assessment feedback. *Teaching in Higher Education* **27** pp. 53–64

Juwah, C., Macfarlane-Dick, D., Matthew, B., Nicol, D., Ross, D. and Smith, B. (2004) *Enhancing Student Learning Through Effective Formative Feedback* HEA Resource Guide. Retrieved 14 March 2010 from http://www.heacademy.ac.uk/resources/detail/resource_data base/id353_effective_formative_feedback_juwah_etal

Leach, L., Neutze, G. & Zepke, N. (2001) Assessment and Empowerment: some critical questions. *Assessment & Evaluation in Higher Education* **26** (4) pp. 293–304

Sadler, D. R. (1983) Evaluation and the improvement of academic learning. *Journal of Higher Education* **54** (1) pp. 60–79

Sadler, D. R. (1989) Formative assessment and the design of instructional systems *Instructional Science* **18** pp. 119–44

Samuelowitz, K. and Bain, J. (2002) Identifying academics' orientations to assessment practice. *Higher Education* **43** (2) pp. 173–201

Torrence, H. & Pryor, J. (1998) *Investigating formative assessment: teaching, learning and assessment in the classroom.* Philadelphia, PA: Open University Press

Whitelock, D. (2009) Editorial: e-assessment: developing new dialogues for the digital age. *British Journal of Educational Technology* **40** (2) pp. 199–202

Yorke, M. (2003) Formative assessment in higher education: Moves towards theory and the enhancement of pedagogic practice. *Higher Education* **45** (4) pp. 477–501

DR STYLIANOS HATZIPANAGOS is the college e-learning coordinator and the head of the e-learning function at King's Learning Institute (KLI) King's College London. He contributes to the development and delivery of KLI's graduate and undergraduate programmes. He has a first degree in physics and MScs in physics education and in information technology.

His research portfolio includes: the design and evaluation of interactive learning environments, innovation in learning and teaching, formative assessment in higher education, e-assessment, usability and evaluation of e-learning environments and microworlds, computer mediated communication and computer supported collaborative work, social software and social networking.

This research was supported by two teaching and research awards received from the Centre for Distance Education of the University of London. A big thanks to Dr Steven Warburton and Dr Ana Lucena who, as members of the project team, contributed to the analysis of the data on which this chapter was based. I am also grateful to Professor Paul Black from King's College and Professor Bob McCormick from the Open University whose comments were extremely helpful in shaping the formative assessment framework this chapter put forward.

5

Co-ordinating dissertations in a shared modular matrix
Reflections on assessment criteria, delivery and marking

Owen Thomas and Richard Tong
Cardiff School of Sport, University of Wales Institute, Cardiff

The management of students' dissertations in higher education is complicated and demanding. This chapter examines how the process is managed in a complex modular matrix in a school which is the largest provider of sport-related programmes in the UK.

Introduction

We intend to give an insight into the various programmes in Cardiff School of Sport (CSS), the student numbers on each programme and how this changed through the period under consideration. We will also detail how these programmes map onto the dissertation module through the variety of disciplines of study available to students undertaking dissertations in the School. A description of the department, the structure and brief history of the module set the context and rationale. Innovations in assessment and delivery of the module are outlined and to conclude we consider possible future innovations.

The study is based on a six-year period between the academic years 2004–05 and 2009–10. The module described is a Level 6, 40-credit module entitled *Undergraduate Dissertation Module*. The module is a compulsory requirement for all students on sport-related honours degrees with CSS. In 2009–10 there were approximately 400 students undertaking dissertations, supervised by over fifty staff. Table 1 provides a synopsis of the programmes of study and the number of students in the CSS who undertook the dissertation module during the study period.

These tables illustrate the growth in student numbers through this period. One of the key aspects of the case study relates to the changes in delivery, supervision and marking needed to enable us to cope with these increased student numbers. As indicated by Armstrong (2004), levels of student dissatisfaction and subsequent student failure can be attributed to inadequacies in the process of dissertation supervision; a factor often exacerbated in programmes with high student numbers.

In the CSS structure, indicative modular content of each programme is delivered

Table 1 The number of students per programme on the module

2004–05		2009–10	
Honours programmes of study	No of students	Honours programmes of study	No of students
BSc Sport and Exercise Science	53	BSc Sport and Exercise Science	112
BSc Sport and Physical Education	106	BSc Sport and Physical Education	92
BSc Sport Coaching	44	BSc Sport Coaching	36
BSc Sport Development	45	BSc Sport Development	46
		BSc Sport Management	19
		BSc Sport Conditioning, Rehabilitation and Massage	13
		BA Dance	81

through a series of *disciplines*, with each discipline having a nominated teaching team. These disciplines underpin the process of supervision in the dissertation module: each student is supervised by a discipline-specific tutor. Undergraduate programme revalidation and organisational change meant that the disciplines were subject to change through the period considered in this case study. Table 2 distinguishes how the discipline structure has changed over this period.

Table 2 The discipline structure over the period of the case study

2004–05	2009–10
Dance	Dance
Biomechanics	Biomechanics
Sport Psychology	Psychology
Sport Physiology	Physiology and Health
Performance Analysis	Performance Analysis
Socio-Cultural	Socio-Cultural
Sport Coaching and Physical Education	Coaching
Sport Development	Management
Sport Injuries	Sport Conditioning Rehabilitation and Massage (SCRAM)
Health and Special Populations	Professional Development

Some historical context: A rationale for change

When the lead author took responsibility for the *Undergraduate Dissertation Module*, the process and product were closely aligned with the model of a traditional dissertation. The assessment criteria and presentation structure of the students' work were very closely related, if not constrained by the boundaries of a traditional quantitative empirical study. Across all disciplines of study dissertations were biased by the work published in the sport and exercise science domains. The assessment criteria were structured around a traditional quantitative empirical paper, with a format designed to separate abstract, introduction, a review of literature, method, results and discussion sections. Given the historical development of the degree programmes within the school, and the previous co-ordinators of the module (the module had been led by a sport and exercise scientist for the preceding ten years) there was a logical explanation for this position. Further, this historical progression was in accordance with the developments in subjects such as bioscience (Luck, 2008).

Concerns had been raised by external examiners, through student feedback and by some discipline groups over the scope and breadth of the assessment criteria for dissertation work. A narrow set of assessment criteria limited the possible learning experience of the students. The criteria did not readily allow for the assessment of qualitative work or dissertations which provided theoretical debate. This was creating a situation in the school where students were seeking to produce such work but the constraints of our assessment criteria were limiting their options. Alternatively, students were producing such studies and tutors were faced with assessing work with criteria unfit for purpose. So one of the early projects was to modify the assessment criteria to encompass the broader range of dissertation 'types' desired in the school, in accordance with the guidance of Walliman (2005). The aim of this process was to broaden the student learning experience through the provision of a more diverse assessment criteria strategy, described below.

The support structures and delivery content of the module are also relevant to the history. Traditionally, individual dissertation tutorials (up to a maximum of 7.5 hours per student) were supplemented with 12 one-hour lecture sessions delivering generic dissertation support in the first 12 teaching weeks of the academic year. These sessions provided information about research ethics and informed consent, organisation and time management, scientific writing skills, dissertation format and structure, research design and data analysis, with students from all disciplines and programmes attending at the same time. This model was similar to that proposed by Burgess (2005) and based on the principles of Morrison et al (2007).

Several issues were apparent from student and staff feedback about these support and delivery modes. The increased student numbers in the school were placing increased demands on individual tutors. Furthermore, the delivery of dissertation support by lectures with simultaneous attendance from all disciplines and programmes prevented the provision of discipline-specific material for the students. This issue had a direct impact on student engagement and subsequent student attendance throughout the 12-week period of lecture support. Student feedback emphasised the lack of content-specific information provided in these sessions; they said this influenced their motivation to attend as they perceived a lack of relevance to their individual topic.

The final process to note here is the marking of students' dissertations. When the lead author took over responsibility for the module, the supervisor marked the product, and dissertations were subsequently moderated in each discipline ('within discipline moderation'). They were then moderated across the disciplines ('cross discipline moderation'). External examiners raised concerns about the objectivity of the first marking process and questioned whether our moderation processes befitted the definition of moderation. Discussions with the external examiners and at the school learning and teaching committee led to an agreement to review the marking processes.

Innovations

Assessment

Through the six academic years we are covering in this chapter our first innovation was to change the assessment criteria to encompass a broader range of dissertation work. Given the rigidity of the assessment criteria in the dissertation module, a series of focus groups were undertaken with the discipline staff groups to find avenues to broaden the types of dissertations available to students. These focus groups confirmed that a broader range of dissertation work was actually being undertaken in the School, but the assessment criteria did not 'fit' all areas of study. This created a situation where tutors were forced to mark the students' work without adhering to the assessment criteria, or were forced to adapt the criteria outside their designed parameters. This was obviously a less than ideal scenario, as noted by the external examiners and student feedback. So a second series of focus groups was held to ascertain the different 'types' of dissertations already existing in the school, in order to create assessment criteria for such work. During these sessions it emerged that greater scope was required in the criteria to allow for the completion and assessment of qualitative research of primary data, and research dealing with secondary data in the form of conceptual or theoretical studies (such as desk based studies, critical review work, meta-analysis). It was agreed in these discussions that assessment of these 'types' of dissertations could occur through the development of new criteria and the manipulation of existing criteria.

A further development specific to the disciplines and programmes of sport management and sport development emerged from these discussions. Some of the learning outcomes of these programmes fitted with the staff's wish to allow dissertation work related to developing a business, so a task group was formed to create a new independent study module (the Enterprise Project) to meet these demands. Collaborative meetings were held with representatives of the Cardiff School of Management, in which dissertation work of this nature was already available. The Enterprise Project module was subsequently validated in the CSS and now acts as a viable independent study module for students on the sport management, sport development and sport and physical education programmes, enhancing the learning of these students through a broader assessment strategy.

Returning to the assessment criteria associated with the dissertation module, a concern was voiced across the focus groups that multiple sets of assessment criteria for the same module would create confusion among students and staff. We still wanted to keep the assessment criteria to a minimum number of sets. Following several further focus group sessions it was agreed that the school would use two differing sets of criteria to assess undergraduate dissertations. These would include a set of assessment criteria for 'empirical' related dissertations, and a set of criteria for 'theoretical/conceptual' related dissertations. In order to allow greater flexibility in these types of dissertations, three sets of descriptors were created for the assessment criteria, which illustrated to students conducting the dissertation and staff marking the work, areas where 'credit would be awarded'. A set of descriptors for 'empirical quantitative dissertations' and a set of descriptors for 'empirical qualitative dissertations' were created to work alongside the empirical assessment criteria. This allowed the specific nuances of these types of studies to emerge, but maintained a consistent application of assessment criteria between the dissertation types.

For example, in the case of qualitative dissertations, the criteria allowed the results and discussion sections to be presented as a combined section followed by an applicable conclusion, or to be presented in a more traditional format of a separate results and discussion section. This same flexibility was not present in dissertations of a quantitative nature which required separate presentation of the results and discussion sections. This increased scope was deemed appropriate for qualitative dissertations, given the number of qualitative peer reviewed research papers that now adopt such presentation methods.

Table 3 Section example of distribution of credit between quantitative and qualitative dissertations

Cardiff School of Sport	**Dissertation Assessment Proforma:** Empirical (Qualitative/Quantitative)

Marking criteria
Results and analysis [1]
Mark allocation ....../15
To include:
❑ description and justification of data treatment/ data analysis procedures
❑ appropriate presentation of analysed data within text and in tables or figures
❑ description of critical findings.

Discussion and Conclusions [1]
Mark allocation ....../30
To include:
❑ collation of information and ideas and evaluation of those ideas relative to the extant literature/concept/theory and research question/problem
❑ adoption of a personal position on the study by linking and combining different elements of the data reported
❑ discussion of the real-life impact of your research findings for coaches and/or practitioners (i.e. practical implications)
❑ discussion of the limitations and a critical reflection of the approach/process adopted
❑ and indication of potential improvements and future developments building on the study
❑ and a conclusion which summarises the relationship between the research question and the major findings.

1   There is scope within qualitative dissertations for the result and discussion sections to be presented as a combined section followed by an appropriate conclusion. The mark distribution and criteria across these two sections should be aggregated in those circumstances

The descriptors for qualitative dissertations outlined the specific areas where credit would be awarded for such dissertations with the assessment criteria outlining differential weightings, depending on the presentation method adopted (that is, results and discussion combined followed by an applicable summary, or separate presentation of results and discussion – see Table 3). A further example related to the content of descriptors across the method sections of quantitative and qualitative dissertations. It was seen as acceptable for these different types of dissertations to be assessed using the same criteria, but it was also considered that the descriptors should reflect slightly different detail in relation to the allocation of marks. For example, issues of trustworthiness apparent in qualitative design were emphasised in the descriptors of such dissertations, whereas this same emphasis was not present in the descriptors of quantitative dissertations (see Table 4).

As a result of this work similar flexibility is now possible between the assessment criteria and the descriptors of theoretical/conceptual types of dissertation. The theoretical/conceptual criteria are used to assess a range of dissertations from meta-analysis dissertations in the more traditional sport and exercise science disciplines

Table 4   Section example of descriptor information across the method sections of quantitative and qualitative dissertations

Cardiff School of Sport	**Dissertation Descriptors:** Empirical (Qualitative/Quantitative)

Descriptors
Method and Research Design (quantitative)
Mark allocation ..../15
Reward in this section should/will be given for:
❑ Appropriateness (i.e., to the research problem/question) and justification of the methods, research design and tools used (e.g. psychometric instrument, validated physiological/biomechanical test – why and how?)
❑ Critical reflection on approach, choice and deployment of design and methods (including those not adopted)
❑ Appropriateness and justification of the interpretative / analytical techniques used
❑ Communication of an awareness of issues of validity/reliability of the adopted method and procedure
❑ Replicability of the study from the information presented.

Descriptors
Method and Research Design (qualitative)
Mark allocation ..../15
Reward in this section should/will be given for:
❑ Appropriateness (i.e., to the research problem/question) and justification of the methods, research design and tools used (e.g. survey, interview, focus groups – why and how?)
❑ Critical reflection on approach and choice and deployment of methods (including those not adopted)
❑ Appropriateness and justification of the interpretative / analytical techniques used
❑ Communication of an awareness of issues of validity/reliability/trustworthiness/bias
❑ Replicability of the study from the information presented.

to theoretical debates and works on conceptual positions in the social sciences. The descriptors associated with these dissertations allow such flexibility to occur under one form of assessment criteria. For example, in conceptual-debate-type dissertations, where reproducibility is not so much of a driving force (in comparison to meta-analysis type dissertations), students can present an extended introduction and refrain from including a separate section outlining the research method and process adopted in the dissertation. The descriptors emphasise the importance of both conceptual-debate dissertations and meta-analysis dissertations alluding to research methods and process, but acknowledge that in the latter these issues are more pertinent; as such, a separate section in the dissertation is warranted. Further, the assessment criteria and descriptors clearly outline to the students and staff how marks should be allocated for the differing modes of presentation of work.

Delivery and support

As noted in the historical context section, several issues acted as the rationale for innovation in the delivery and support of the dissertation module. These related to the growing number of students on the module and the subsequent demands placed on supervisors and, a lack of student engagement and attendance during the formal taught contact elements of the generic dissertation support. Over the course of the case study period, several innovations were undertaken to try to counter these problems. Following several focus group sessions and discussion at the school learning and teaching committee, an overarching goal was drawn up to establish a more context specific delivery of the taught elements of the dissertation module. Early in the case study period (i.e. 2004–06), attempts to attain this goal focused around shortening the generic dissertation support to the first eight weeks of term. This was supplemented by workshops looking at the analysis of quantitative and qualitative data. Students were required to attend the session related to their dissertation type. It was initially anticipated that these analysis sessions would increase student engagement as they fell close to the period when students were beginning to think about analysing their data. However, when these changes were made across the two cohorts, there was little change in the engagement of students and attendance remained poor.

Student feedback provided several explanations for this. Although the students who attended the analysis workshops found them worthwhile, there still remained an underlying perception by the students that these sessions lacked context across all disciplines. The students noted that there was still a bias in presentation during these sessions. For example, if a sport physiologist delivered the quantitative workshop programme there was a natural bias towards that discipline in the examples provided in the session, and students from other disciplines did not identify with the context of the delivery. Moreover, these early modifications were not making the supervision provided by staff in the school more efficient, as many students still required in-depth support during analysis of data.

In response, we decided that, for the academic year 2007–08, students would receive six weeks of generic dissertation support followed by two discipline-specific group-tutorial sessions in the remaining six weeks of term one. The generic quantitative and qualitative workshops were removed from the module teaching schedule and replaced by separate discipline-led sessions. It was hoped that delivering dissertation support at a the level of a discipline would release the specific content information that the students wanted and also offset some of the pressure for support on supervisors as student numbers increased (see Table 1).

Several messages could be communicated to groups of students rather than being repeated through a series of up to 10 individual dissertation tutorials. In collaboration with their respective teaching teams, the discipline directors provided these sessions; one session focused on research questions, design and method and the second on writing and analysis of data. These sessions appeared to more readily engage the students and resulted in higher levels of attendance through 2007–08. They received positive feedback at module evaluation stage, and the students made comments to the external examiners on the good impact of these sessions. As such, the support format outlined above continued for the academic year 2008–09, with similarly positive outcomes. Indeed, the staff discipline groups commented favourably on these sessions and the increased ownership they felt over the dissertation process in their domain. The staff also provided feedback on the ability of these sessions to communicate key messages common to the dissertation process effectively in a discipline specific context. They saw this as an important advance in effective use of their time as a supervisor.

Further, they noted an improved opportunity for peer learning among the students in the discipline and observed the active discussions that often took place in these group-based sessions, benefiting a range of students. In recognition of this, some disciplines took the opportunity for several staff members to attend the session rather than relying on the discipline director to deliver alone. Given the increased ownership the discipline groups felt, and the impact of these sessions on staff perceptions of efficient supervision, staff members were happy to attend these sessions. This resulted in small breakout groups being used in the discipline specific support sessions through 2008–09. For example, in the sport psychology sessions, students formed separate breakout groups based on whether they were undertaking a qualitative or quantitative dissertation. This enabled an even deeper context to be provided to these students with regard to analysis of data and writing of the dissertation, but still allowed peer learning and discussion to take place, thus fostering a sharing of issues in the relevant student population.

The positive impact of this delivery method was further enhanced for the academic year 2009–10. Following the positive reception of these sessions by student and staff groups, and the favourable response noted in external examiner reports, each discipline ran three discipline specific sessions through the 2009–10 academic year. The module started with four generic dissertation-support sessions in the first four teaching weeks of term, covering aspects related to supervisor allocation, delineation of dissertation types (marking pro forma and descriptors), ethics and informed consent, academic writing and plagiarism. During the remaining seven teaching weeks in the run up to the Christmas break, each discipline group received two discipline-specific sessions. These covered the research question, design, method and academic writing. Each discipline also ran a specific support session after the Christmas break, on analysis and presentation of data. Feedback on this approach is yet to be collected, but it is anticipated that the delivery style will continue to receive positive responses from the groups involved.

Marking and moderation

Here we discuss the innovations made to marking and moderation procedures. As pointed out at the beginning of this chapter, the student's supervisor marked the student's dissertation, and the dissertations then passed through 'within discipline' and 'cross discipline' moderation exercises. All staff supervising dissertations attended a 'cross discipline' meeting. The external examiners were always highly complimentary of the philosophy underpinning this approach, and noted it as strength of the school's moderation processes. However, staff commented in their feedback that there was sometimes a tension apparent at these open meetings, because individual staff perceived that they had to justify their marks to colleagues. Additionally, the increased staff numbers in the school were creating logistical issues in the efficient and effective running of the exercise. In response to these issues, several innovations in practice were introduced.

Following consultation, it was agreed that for the academic year 2005–06 'cross discipline' moderation would involve only discipline directors rather than the entire teaching team. In 2006–07 the process was modified further so that disciplines with common approaches could moderate each other's work. Additionally, the guidelines of the cross-discipline exercise were altered so that we ensured that the broad classification of award was comparable across the disciplines (that is, to within five per cent), shifting away from a focus on individual grades. Discipline directors were charged with the responsibility of disseminating information to their discipline teams with respect to any issues associated with the marking processes and feedback provided on the marking pro forma to students. Staff in the school approved these changes, so the ethos associated with the cross-discipline moderation process remained when dissertation work was assessed. The external examiners commented that the process was now more aligned with 'true' moderation and provided positive comments on the cross-moderation process.

Changes to the first marking process were adopted through 2006–07 and although double-blind marking was considered, it was decided that first marking and within-discipline moderation were preferable. The within-discipline moderation gave new and experienced staff an opportunity to share ideas and learn from their peers about assessing students' work. Several discipline groups noted that important discussions took place at these discipline specific moderation exercises, a benefit which would be lost were within-discipline moderation to be removed, or if the School adopted double-blind first marking followed by cross-discipline moderation.

However, the learning and teaching committee were aware of the external examiners' comments on the objectivity of first marking. So, following discussion, the school's first marking procedure was altered. Students' dissertations were marked by an independent academic member of staff from the discipline of study rather than by their supervisor. Following this first marking, the mark awarded was discussed by the marker and supervisor. If there was a discrepancy between the mark and the dissertation supervisor's perceptions of the work in the supervisory process (reading of draft work, tutor-student discussions), the dissertation was raised as a specific case to be reviewed at the within-discipline moderation.

Future innovations and conclusions

Several other innovations are under consideration for the dissertation module. Some of the more performance and application-related disciplines – Sports Coaching, Dance, Sport Conditioning Rehabilitation and Massage (SCRAM) – have expressed a desire for their students to engage in a performance-related dissertation. While this has been undertaken in some of the performing arts disciplines (e.g. Calvert & Casey, 2004), further development is required to take this forward in a sporting context. Although the idea is in its infancy, early impressions indicate that this type of dissertation could take the form of a performance followed by a reflective narrative account of the process. This type of dissertation would, for example, allow a sport-coaching student to undertake fieldwork followed by a reflective narrative of the process. A separate set of criteria and descriptors would be needed to assess dissertations of this type. Following the success of greater ownership over the delivery of dissertation support, there is a desire in the School to explore other avenues to maximise the effectiveness and efficiency of this type of delivery.

In conclusion, this chapter has presented a reflective account of several modifications to the assessment and delivery of a large undergraduate dissertation module. It is hoped that readers will have been able to empathise with the challenges and issues faced by the CSS, and the authors hope that by sharing our innovations we may assist colleagues faced with similar situations in their deliberations on delivery and assessment of independent work. Finally, the authors suggest that if providing a dissertation support module, staff should consider the approaches presented in this chapter but should not neglect the generic guidance that is available from other sources (such as Cullen, 2009).

References

Armstrong, S. (2004) The impact of supervisor's cognitive styles on the quality of research supervision in management education. *British Journal of Educational Psychology* 74 pp. 599–616

Burgess, C. (2005) *Managing undergraduate dissertations. A case study.* At http://www.heacademy. ac.uk/hlst/resources/casestudies/dissertations/ Visited 3 October 2009

Calvert, B. and Casey, B. (2004) Supporting and assessing dissertations and practical projects in media studies degrees: Towards collaborative learning. *Art Design and Communication in Higher Education* 3 47–60

Cullen, S. (2009) *Resource guide to dissertation supervision on taught undergraduate and postgraduate programmes.* At http://www.heacademy.ac.uk/assets/hlst/documents/resource_guides/dissertation_supervision.pdf/ Visited 28 September 2009

Luck, M. (2008) *Student research projects: Guidance on practice in the biosciences.* At http://www. bioscience.heacademy.ac.uk/resources/guides/studentres.aspx/ Visited 3 October 2009

Morrison, J., Oladunjoye, G. and Onyefulu, C. (2007) An assessment of research supervision: A leadership model enhancing current practices in business and management. *Journal of Education for Business* 82 (4) 212–19

Walliman, N. (2005) *Your Dissertation: The Essential Guide for Success.* Sage Publications: London.

DR OWEN THOMAS is a senior lecturer in sport psychology in the Cardiff School of Sport at the University of Wales Institute, Cardiff. He is a published researcher across the sport psychology domains of competitive stress, sports confidence and psychological skill use and is associate editor of the *European Journal of Sport Science.* Dr Thomas is chartered with the British Psychological Society and accredited with the British Association of Sport and Exercise Sciences. He primarily teaches aspects of sport psychology across undergraduate and post-graduate modules, leads the UG dissertation module and is the discipline director for research methods at PG level in the school.

DR RICHARD TONG is the director of learning & teaching and deputy dean in the Cardiff School of Sport at UWIC. He is also the sport liaison officer for the H E Academy Subject Centre for Hospitality, Leisure, Sport and Tourism. He is the chair of the Education & Professional Development Division for the British Association of Sport & Exercise Science and the moderator champion for learning & teaching for the University of Wales. His research interests and publications are in sports physiology, pedagogy and assessment.

6

Feed-forward
Supporting transferable skills with formative feedback

Diane Rushton, Louise Sparshatt, and Rona O'Brien
Sheffield Hallam University

This chapter describes a project to support students' autonomous learning skills by providing formative feedback or 'feed-forward' on their achievement of transferable skills – on their use of English, research or analysis – rather than on their success in applying the module content in the assessment.

Introduction

For feed-forward to be truly effective, students must engage with it while they are undertaking their work. By breaking down the assessment criteria into understandable guidance about how to achieve the criteria *before* students completed their work, the assessment of how far students had achieved the criteria was then developed into a reflective self-assessment process between tutor and student. The process promoted engagement with the assessment criteria and also helped the tutor pick up on general areas of weakness in generic skills such as referencing. Students demonstrated improvement in their assessment and their engagement with feedback.

This chapter describes a project that ran with two Level 5 modules in a business studies degree to support students' autonomous learning skills by providing formative feedback, or feed-forward, on their achievement of transferable skills, i.e. on their use of English, research, or analysis, rather than success in applying the module content in the assessment. By feed-forward we mean that the feedback given can be used directly into the next module assignments as students are assessed again in those skill areas. Furthermore, as the feed-forward relates to transferable skills, students can feed this forward into other modules. An important message to get across to students was the transferability of core skills and the fact that these are just as important as subject knowledge. How information is researched, analysed and written plays a key role in ensuring the right subject knowledge is used and communicated.

Students stated that they found it difficult to recognise or untangle feed-forward from feedback. A pilot project was started to trial the use of a form to provide specific formative feed-forward based on the skills assessment criteria. But the team believed that, for feed-forward to be truly effective, students must engage with it while they are undertaking their work, rather than it being a retrospective activity and the process was developed to work over a number of assessments during the semester.

We used the assessment criteria to create understandable guidance about how to achieve the criteria *before* students completed their work. The assessment of how far students had achieved the criteria was then developed into a reflective self-assessment process between tutor and student.

Potential issues with student engagement, because this was not how they were used to receiving feedback, were addressed by the module leader introducing feed-forward as the accepted way of giving feedback in this module, with no special emphasis on the process. Students immediately paid more attention to the assessment criteria. It promoted engagement and also helped the tutor pick up on general areas of weakness in generic skills such as referencing. Students demonstrated improvement in their assessment and their engagement with feedback and appreciated the fact that they were being helped to help themselves.

Objectives

The project was developed as a method of supporting and enhancing students as autonomous learners by providing feedback specifically aimed at describing their success or areas of development in terms of transferable skills, to be applied throughout their academic career.

The feed-forward process developed initially was refined on the basis of feedback from students, and an assessment of the level of engagement with the feed-forward from students. The process was designed to complement existing approaches to feedback, rather than replace them, as it was discovered from initial exploratory discussions with students that this feed-forward element of feedback was often missing.

The provision of effective feed-forward skills-related feedback – and the introduction of an element of self-assessment by students, underpinned by the participation of students and staff – was also intended to develop staff's assessment practice by encouraging them to consciously separate skills-based feedback from content-based feedback. It should also allow students to easily make use of the relevant skills-based feedback, as students said that they could find it difficult to recognise and separate the two elements of feedback.

As the project developed it was necessary to understand clearly how the process did and did not work, so that it could be easily applied by other members of staff and to disseminate the findings of the project to other faculties within the university, and more widely in the sector.

Rationale

There has been a focus on the provision of feedback to students at Sheffield Hallam

University, as elsewhere in the sector, since the launch of the National Student Survey in 2005. Research undertaken in the university (O'Brien and Sparshatt, 2007) showed that students would like to use assessment feedback for future learning and assessments; however, while staff appreciate the need for feed-forward, they believe that students' main concern is with the mark (Smith and Gorard, 2005; Randall and Mirador, 2003) and that students do not appreciate that their feedback is useful for future work in any module (O'Brien and Sparshatt, 2007).

This project began with an alternative view, that students may find it difficult to untangle feed-forward from feedback, and that staff may not prioritise providing feed-forward comments (Smith and Gorard, 2005; Duncan 2007: 276; Taras 2006), especially when experiencing workload pressure. When tested via a short questionnaire at the beginning of the trial, a majority of students (58 out of 95) said they believed they usually received feedback that concentrated purely on the content of the work and did not provide help with the generic skills to take forward into future learning.

An initial pilot trialled the provision of specific feed-forward based on the assessment criteria. By assessing the students on the same assessment criteria throughout the module, they would have the opportunity to respond to the feedback and develop in these areas. The development in transferable skills would help them improve their performance, not only in this module, but across modules and would be important for the development of employability skills.

Context

The two modules involved were:

Managing in a Global Context (One tutor / 100 students)
❑ A core Level 5 module for students on the HND Business and Finance programme
❑ A core Level 5 module for the students on BA International Business and BA International Business and Language
❑ An option module for students on a variety of business degree programmes within the school

Globalisation and Business (Two tutors / 30 students)
❑ A core module on the part-time HNC and part-time degree Business and Management.

The part-time students are taught in mixed groups including students in their 1st, 2nd and 3rd semester of Level 5 (taught over 18 months). They therefore have a wide and different level of transferable core skills. The project was limited to the seminar groups of the module leader, with the intention of rolling it out should it be successful.

As a result of revalidation the opportunity arose to adopt a fresh approach to the teaching, learning and assessment in two modules. Previous experience of teaching on Level 5 modules made it apparent that students did not see the link between assessment criteria and feedback and how it could be used as feed-forward to improve their future work. The module leader wanted to find a way to raise the standard, importance and value of feed-forward and to ensure that students used the feed-forward to enhance their learning.

Previously the modules were assessed through one piece of coursework, an essay, and a three-essay exam. The feedback given to students on the coursework essay seemed to be largely ignored or forgotten in the exam essays, which showed little evidence of research or referencing, and lacked structure and critical analysis. The assessment model was changed to three/four pieces of linked coursework with no exam, to enable the feed-forward process to be effective.

In order for the feed-forward to be of maximum use to students they were assessed as far as possible by the same assessment criteria, on each piece of work. Working in collaboration with an expert from the University Learning and Teaching Institute, subject and skills-based assessment criteria were drawn up that were transferable between the different types of assessment (see Figure 1).

Table 1: The assessment criteria *

| | Assignment Format | | | |
Criteria	Web-exercise	Presentation	Report Proposal	Report
Analysis	✗			✗
Research	✗	✗	✗	✗
Communication	✗		✗	✗
Content /theory			✗	✗
Reflection	✗			

* see appendix for detail

The assessment (see Table 2) consisted of three pieces of coursework for the full-time students.

❑ Assessment one: web-based exercise 30%
❑ Assessment two: report proposal 20%
❑ Assessment three: report 50%

For the part-time students, this consisted of four pieces of coursework:

❑ Assessment one: web-based exercise 20%
❑ Assessment two: presentation 10%
❑ Assessment three: report proposal 20%
❑ Assessment four: report 50%.

Table 2 Briefing and feed-forward process

Assignment	Briefing	Hand in	Feedback and feed-forward
1	week 1	week 4	week 7 in class session
2	week 4	week 8	week 11 in class session
3	week 4	week 15 after teaching has finished	week 18 students can collect from reception

Description

The research team started with the idea of giving students a simple form based on the assessment criteria alongside their feedback, to highlight where they needed to improve generic skills and where they already had well-developed skills. The feedback following the initial trial showed that the inclusion of positive feedback was particularly welcomed by students. However, adding an indicator of the level of achievement would make the form more useful, and discussions showed that the assessment criteria underpinning the judgments in the form could be opaque to students.

For the second year the methodology was significantly reworked to attempt to give students a deeper understanding of what was expected of them and to encourage self-reflection. A new form broke down the assessment criteria into terms that were understandable, to answer students' complaints about the opaque language, and to give students firm guidance about how to achieve the criteria *before* they completed their work.

The second development to ensure engagement of students in the process was to assess how far students had achieved the criteria (now graded into 'fully achieved', 'partially achieved' and 'not achieved') into a reflective self-assessment process. After completion of their work, students were asked to assess how far they felt they had achieved the criteria. When the work had been marked they received the form back with the tutor's assessment of their success alongside their own assessment and were able to compare the two. The hand-back seminar was a vital part of this process; the tutor talked to each student about their work and how far they had achieved the criteria, so that the student fully understood why they might have over- or underestimated their success in achieving the skills criteria.

The effectiveness of the approach was tested in two ways, by the students' perception of its success and by the tutor's judgement of any visible improvement in the students' work.

Evaluation

Early stages of the project

During the first semester of the trial in 2008, some issues were encountered with the method of encouraging the students to work with transferable skills. After the first piece of work was handed back, one student formally asked to be withdrawn from the research project; their reason was that they were only interested in content and not skills development. The concerns of the part-time students were expressed by this student: that, as a Level 5 part-time student who had spent six semesters at the university, they felt that they did not need feed-forward on transferable skills as they knew how to research and write. It had to be made clear that we were not questioning their writing ability *per se*, but their ability to write at an academic level appropriate for Level 5. The feed-forward was to help them develop and improve their academic writing and other transferable skills, in particular to enable them to progress through Levels 5 and 6 effectively.

The other area of concern for the students was that they felt that discussion about transferable skills was taking away time in the seminar that should be focused on *content*. One of the reasons for this was their feedback on previous and other modules were purely focused on content. These concerns were echoed by the full-time students.

When the research team considered the feedback from students, they concluded that the different levels of experience of being a part-time Level 5 student had not been fully recognised. By carefully introducing the feed-forward in order to ensure the students were comfortable with the process, an unintended consequence was that the students saw feed-forward as an add-on, rather than an integrated part of the module. They just wanted to be told how to pass rather than reflect on their own ability and use feed-forward to improve it.

It appeared that the focus was too much on ensuring that the students of the lowest ability were not intimidated by the self-assessment process and the students of higher ability were alienated as a result, as the most vocal students were those that had achieved high marks on previous modules and were expecting high marks on this module and were disappointed with their lower marks. The emphasis on the research may have allowed them to focus their discontent about their performance on that, rather than addressing their own issues. In contrast, the weaker students seemed to appreciate the additional support provided by the feed-forward and engaged in discussion with the tutor about it.

Addressing the issues and developing a successful process

Following consideration of this student feedback, in semester two the feed-forward was introduced to the students by the tutor to ensure that the barriers discussed above were removed. The feed-forward was introduced briefly to students as a natural part of the course by the tutor and students were left to work with it without special induction into how to self-assess. Students were given their first feed-forward in the briefing for assignment one (see Table 2) so that they could immediately self-assess and reflect on their skills, and be more involved in the process. The results were positive: students were not intimidated by the thought of self-assessment and appreciated both the up-front help of the breakdown of the assessment criteria included on the form, an innovation in their academic career, and the chance to learn more about the expectations of the tutor via the comparison of self-evaluation and tutor-evaluation. The discussion with the tutor was an important part of the process that was especially valued by students.

Student evaluation of the process

In the first semester, when students received their first piece of marked coursework with the feed-forward, the two researchers came in to facilitate the session. The discussions with students showed that they found it difficult to understand how they could use the feed-forward in their next assignment because the content was going to be different. In this session they were given the feed-forward for the next assignment so that they could complete the self-evaluation and submit it with their work. Despite reassurances, many were concerned that their self-assessment would influence the marker.

However, as assignment two and three were linked with assessment criteria focusing on the same core skills of research and communication, when they received their feed-forward from assignment two students clearly saw how this could have a positive impact on their final piece of work if they reflected and applied it to their next piece of work. It was noticeable that the majority of students had improved the range of sources utilised, the level of writing, their analysis, and adopted the Harvard system of referencing in the final report. The tutor noted that the introduction of the approach made students think more carefully about feed-forward, the importance of transferable skills and the integration between subject knowledge and communication.

An additional advantage of the process was that it helped the tutor pick up on any areas of skills weakness. In the briefing on assignment one, students assessed themselves as needing to develop their referencing. This was borne out by their first assignment, so the Harvard system of referencing was explained to them. As a result many students then assessed themselves as 'good'. From sessions with students it was clear that they were beginning to understand the importance of developing and improving these transferable skills in their work. By assignment three, many students had the confidence to assess themselves as 'excellent'. The tutor was able to concur with the students' self-assessment. In comparison with their previous work, the tutor found that the majority of the students had improved in research sources, referencing, academic writing and critical analysis.

Discussion

The development of the feed-forward process was positive; the research team learned a great deal about how students want to learn and as a result developed a process to help them. The development of the process depended on the feedback from students being accepted and constructively acted upon, even when it challenged preconceptions about how students learn. However, as the project was concerned with helping students to actively use feedback, the research team needed to engage in a similar process.

Feedback from students was blunt, and at times negative, but almost always constructive. For example, students commented that it would be more helpful if the additional information about the criteria could be more specific to the assessment task. It was also clear that the majority of students valued the increased guidance on their development and the opportunity to discuss this with the tutor. A caveat is that the feed-forward process must not interfere with what the students perceive to be the reason they are on the course, which is to learn the course content. By developing a methodology that slipped under the radar of the students but still allowed them to feel supported, a positive response to the feed-forward process was elicited.

The development of the assessment criteria was a key part of the process. One of the reasons for including research as an assessment criterion was that students were overly reliant on the core text, Wikipedia and Google. By emphasising the importance of academic research, and through the use of the web exercises, students began to have more confidence in exploring other sources such as subject relevant sites like the World Trade Organisation. It was noticeable in the final report that the majority of students had accessed at least ten sources and some significantly more. Only a few however had taken the step to use academic journals. There still appears to be some fear of accessing or using these. This will be addressed in the next academic year.

An issue to be investigated in the future is that some students expressed an unwillingness to mark themselves highly, as they did not want to be told that they were not as good as they thought they were. This is possibly because the feed-forward elements related to relatively high-stakes assessment. A potential solution to be explored is to ask students to do more self-evaluation in a 'safe' context, so that they are more willing to be honest with themselves.

A caveat for the whole process and the way in which the success of the project was evaluated is necessary at this point. Although the perceptions of the tutor who marked the students' work of the improvement in the standard of work in these areas of transferable skills is an important indicator, it is not possible to substantiate this with a quantitative improvement to marks as several other factors influence the quality of students' work. The feed-forward was focused on core skills and though the module leader can say they improved, in terms of content some students were still lacking.

However, the process as it stands has demonstrated benefits for students in allowing them more confidence in working with and achieving assessment criteria that describe generic skills. The final process requires dedication from the tutor but repays this effort, as students demonstrate improvement and appreciate the fact that they are being helped to help themselves.

Lessons learned

The following are some of the main learning points from the project:

❑ Students value the additional guidance provided on the assessment criteria and discussion with the tutor. The assessment criteria have to be very clear.

❑ If it is to work, feed-forward must be a part of the normal processes of the module or students will feel that it distracts from the time they have to work on the module content. It has to be integrated with the content.

❑ The seminars which include handing back work and discussion of the students' self-assessments should be built into the seminar plan.

❑ The discussion with students is a vital part of the process.

❑ The process as a whole relies on engagement from the tutor to work effectively.

References

Duncan, N. (2007) Feed-forward: Improving students' use of tutors' comments. *Assessment and Evaluation in Higher Education* 32 (3) 271–83

O'Brien, R. and Sparshatt, L. (2007) Mind the gap! Staff perceptions of student perceptions of assessment feedback. *Higher Education Academy 2007 Annual Conference papers*, D7, http://www.heacademy.ac.uk/events/conference/papers

Randall, M. and Mirador, J. (2003) 'How well am I doing? Using a corpus-based analysis to investigate tutor and institutional messages in comment sheets. *Assessment and Evaluation in Higher Education* 28 (5) 515–26

Smith, E. and Gorard, S. (2005) 'They don't give us our marks': the role of formative feedback in student progress. *Assessment in Education* 12 (1) 21–38

Taras, M. (2006) Do unto others or not: equity in feedback for undergraduates. *Assessment and Evaluation in Higher Education* 31 (3) 365–77

DIANE RUSHTON is a Senior Lecturer in International Business at Sheffield Business School. Her research interests are in the area of student assessment and feedback and developing student writing skills.

LOUISE SPARSHATT is a Senior Officer at Sheffield Hallam University, working in quality enhancement; she has a particular interest in exploring and addressing the issues behind National Student Survey and external examiner data with academic colleagues.

RONA O'BRIEN is Head of Department for Finance Accounting and Business Systems at Sheffield Hallam University; she is involved in several projects involving the student learning experience and in developing and implementing university policy.

Appendix: Feed forward feedback form

This section describes how to achieve the assessment criteria. You are required to evaluate your work and judge how far you have achieved the criteria according to the description by ticking the appropriate boxes.

When your work is returned your tutor will have added how far you have achieved the criteria. It is recommended that you examine this feedback, especially where your view of your work differs from that of the tutor, and use the guidance to inform future pieces of work. The tutor's feedback will highlight those areas that you should concentrate on in the future.

These criteria relate only to skills; you will receive separate feedback on the content of your assignment and it is the combination of your application of skills and the content of your work that is taken into account in your mark.

	Your view			Marker's view		
	Well developed	Partly achieved	Needs developing	Well developed	Partly achieved	Needs developing

Content and Theory

Relevant and comprehensive subject matter

Your choice of material supports what you are saying. You linked relevant theory and concepts of practice. Real-life examples illustrate the point you are making. informative discussion of the topic e.g. *"the HL company example shows what can be done when other companies have faced with these kinds of issues other examples such as the GH company suggests that the company might like to follow HLs example'.*

You have demonstrated creativity and rigour

You cover the majority of the concepts, ideas and theories covered in the lecture.

You have introduced some concepts ideas and theories not covered in the lecture or seminar.

Analysis

Analysis of relevant issues with synthesis of theory and practice

You have sufficiently broken down the given situation or problem into its constituent parts and separated and categorised the information.

You have then applied frameworks or models to all/some of that information so it can be used in a structured way for better decision making. e.g. *a company is trying to understand 'why' it is not doing well in the international marketplace – you may suggest that it conduct an analysis of its environment by using a framework that enables it to scan its environment in a structured way and manage the resulting information by separating it into the categories of Political, Economic, Social, Technological, Environmental and Legal factors. Using these categories the company can make connections; look for patterns in the information to see how*

	Well developed	Partly achieved	Needs developing	Well developed	Partly achieved	Needs developing
		Your view			Marker's view	

Theory and concepts with explained, relevant application to the task set

You have applied and explained relevant frameworks or models to the topic/question in order to make connections and look for patterns across the data, e.g. *you have clearly discussed the concept of globalisation in terms of its impact on International Business*

Provided an argued and convincing case

You refer to academic theories and/or frameworks which you then use to illustrate the point that you are making. Your points have real world relevance and allow you to draw convincing conclusions.

Written communication

Well structured, cohesive and well argued

You focus on the question; each point you make is relevant to your discussion of the topic.

You have a clear introduction followed by discussion and analysis in the main body of the text and a conclusion which sums up the main points.

Your paragraphs are of an appropriate length, addressing a specific point, and your sentences are not over long, or too short to be meaningful.

An acceptable standard of written English

You have an appropriate academic writing style, e.g. – you have used the third person where you should, – *'The author/writer suggests that the organisation should use ...'*

Your writing is concise, understandable and appropriate for the audience.

Your use of punctuation and grammar is accurate and helps the work to be read and understood.

Your spelling is accurate and you have used a range of appropriate vocabulary.

Referencing is thorough and complete with all sources acknowledged

You have correctly used the Harvard referencing system.

You have provided a comprehensive bibliography and reference list.

You used appropriate acknowledgements and referencing in the text.

	Well developed	Partly achieved	Needs developing	Well developed	Partly achieved	Needs developing
		Your view			Marker's view	
Identifying research Sources	The majority of these categories have been used by you: ¶ peer-reviewed journals ¶ academic journals ¶ up-to-date academic textbooks ¶ credible websites ¶ newspapers. ¶ trade-journals ¶ primary sources i.e. first-hand.					
Using research sources	Your research material gives focus to your answer and effectively supports/illustrates what you are saying, e.g: *'this journal article emphasises the points made above and supports the argument that …'*					

7

Using e-portfolio as a reflective assessment tool

Pauline A. Gordon
Queen Margaret University, Edinburgh

This chapter discusses the experience of using e-portfolios as an assessment tool and their role in improving learning and teaching, for second-year hospitality management students. It highlights the management of the introduction of e-portfolios and issues encountered during the implemention of this successful project.

Introduction

Individualised Support for Learning through e-Portfolios (ISLE) is a collaborative project which is funded and managed on behalf of the Scottish Funding Council (SFC). This project aims to transform the experience of students through innovative approaches to teaching and learning. Initially, the project was led by Paisley University and the partner institutions included, Abertay University, Adam Smith College, Angus College, Ayr College, Bell College of Technology, Dumfries and Galloway College, James Watt College Motherwell College and Queen Margaret University (QMU).

This definition helps to clarify any confusion that may exist over e-portfolios:

> an e-portfolio is a product, created by a learner, a collection of digital artefacts articulating experiences, achievements and learning which have benefits in personal development planning (PDP) and models of learning, teaching and assessment. (Beetham, 2005: 1)

In the same work, Beetham states that there seems to be more understanding, particularly in terms of the benefits that e-portfolios may bring to PDP and models of learning, teaching and assessment. Gray further suggests,

> that behind any product, or presentation, lie rich and complex processes of planning, synthesising, sharing, discussing, reflecting, giving, receiving and responding to feedback. (Gray, 2008: 6)

This reinforces the view that e-portfolios have the potential to promote learning and encourage personal development and digital identity by supporting the learning process, the product of learning and the transition of learners at various stages of the lifelong and life-wide journey. (Barrett and Carney, 2005; ISLE, 2005; JISC, 2008; Ward and Grant, 2007)

Over the past decade there has been increasing interest in the potential of e-portfolios to support more student-centred and personalised forms of learning. This has been encouraged by national strategies for e-learning, the Scottish Funding Council, the QAA and other initiatives in support of lifelong and personalised learning. The benefits that electronic portfolios may bring to PDP and the benefits gained from these types of models of learning, teaching and assessment were the primary drivers behind QMU's decision to become an institutional partner in this collaborative project.

Context

Although initiatives and national policies can drive forward new ideas, these still need to be implemented at operational level. Initially, the management of the ISLE project e-portfolio was administered by the Centre of Academic Practice (CAP) at QMU which promoted its benefits, encouraged its use and enabled its effective practice among the various schools. Staff personal development planning led the way in the use of e-portfolios, but this was quickly extended into student assessment and feedback.

I was an early adopter of e-portfolios when they became a voluntary part of the assessment for the postgraduate certificate in higher education, and embraced the technology, particularly given the fact that the University and the School of Business, Enterprise and Management were encouraging its use.

While experience has since demonstrated that the use and implementation of e-portfolios is challenging, it has also proven to be extremely rewarding for staff and students. According to Nickelson (2004), e-portfolios may help educators to reflect on course content and teaching methods. Equally the use of e-portfolios in assessment increases student reflection (Van Sickle et al, 2005: 497). Their use also helps students to become more active and take a greater role in assessment and their own learning as a whole (Corwin, 2003). Thus, one of the most significant reasons for my own use of e-portfolios with students was the way these tools can promote more profound methods of learning, teaching and assessment; there was potential to develop e-portfolios further in the Business School at QMU. This chapter discusses my experience of implementing the e-portfolio into a module and the benefits and problems encountered when implementing this technology.

Discussion

Students enrolled on the International Hospitality Management Programme at QMU are required to complete a second-year module (SCQF Level 8) called *Food and Beverage Project Management*. It consists of practical work sessions and theoretical sessions. The aim of the module is to encourage students to demonstrate achievement through collecting evidence, recording their own progress and setting targets, embracing a continuous process of personal development and reflecting on their own learning. The assessment requires students to critically reflect upon their own learning and submit their e-portfolio through the assessment gateway.

The practical experience provides students with the opportunity to work with a kitchen/front of house team and practise and attain essential skills in a professional environment. The rationale behind the experience is to familiarise students with real working environments and to further help them develop and refine their competences and scope of practice. These practical sessions are an essential learning component for any hospitality degree programme.

While undertaking these practical sessions all students are required to keep updated reflective diaries or records of their learning experience. The first part of the assessment deals with the collection and recording of evidence in the kitchen or restaurant management sessions, which encourages students to reflect on and analyse their own learning performance. The second part of the assessment continues the process of personal development by asking students to reflect in their own diaries and then use the lectures, tutorials and literature to reflect on their own learning and find better or different ways of improving their competences as a manager.

Previously, students were asked to prepare a reflective portfolio on their studies and discuss the key elements of their practical sessions using the lecture/tutorials and literature. However, there were a number of issues highlighted through student feedback. For example, the diary was in paper form and students did not always keep up to date, mainly because the diary was forgotten until the actual assessment day approached. Apart from asking students every week to produce their diaries in class, I had no other way of verifying if they were keeping up to date, and it was easy for them to say that they had forgotten to bring their diaries to campus. In addition, students did not seem to understand what was expected of them in terms of reflecting on their work and using the lecture, tutorials and literature to reflect on that learning. It was therefore decided to consider an alternative assessment tool for the Food and Beverage Project Management module which was the e-portfolio.

Despite realising that the learning, teaching and assessment of this module demanded change, I had reservations about eliminating the aim of the module, which was to encourage students to demonstrate that they could critically reflect upon their own learning and wanted to ensure that students understood what they were supposed to be achieving.

The rationale for implementing the e-portfolio as a new assessment tool was to try and achieve these aims by providing students with the appropriate tools that would help them to represent their 'personal learning journeys' via electronic media. I wanted to upgrade and modernise an outdated module by combining traditional teaching practices such as reflection on an individual's learning with the use of modern technology to improve the opportunity of success. However, I did not want to just use the e-portfolio for the assessment, I wanted to integrate the technology throughout the module. I felt that it had to be reflected in the content and not just be perceived by students as being an extra or additional work.

Example of an e-portfolio

The main page of the e-portfolio is similar to the main body of a paper portfolio. There are different sections within the e-portfolio, but it is much easier to move around the different sections by simply clicking on the area of your choice. There are various links throughout the sections which direct the reader to blogs/diaries or journal articles that have been referred to in lectures.

As can be seen from Figure 1 the e-portfolio has a number of tools which can help students to design their own activities and to record and reflect on their abilities and achievements. For example, by using the Ability tool students can record specific skills and knowledge gained while undertaking the *Food and Beverage Management* module. In the Meeting section students can also record meetings such as study groups and reflect on who did what and who did not contribute to the group. There is also an Action plan tool to help students plan for their future learning.

Figure 1 Example of available e-portfolio tools

What enabled the practice to work?

One of the most crucial aspects of enabling this activity to work was reflecting on my own learning experience with e-portfolios during my post graduate certificate in teaching in higher education. I was not the most organised or dedicated of students and my engagement with the e-portfolio was embarrassingly poor, as I only attended two of the workshops explaining the practicalities and approaches to using the e-portfolio. I was extremely frustrated and disappointed in myself for not obtaining the best learning experience and for not building up practical skills with the technology.

That said, after an abundance of perseverance and once I did manage to master my way around the e-portfolio system, I was pleasantly surprised at the results. I had designed my own private learning place, where I could present a range of artefacts (photos, scanned graphics and text) that discuss my professional learning journey since starting the module and teaching in higher education. I was also able to construct a personal 'profile' and attach a collation of materials from a variety of both formal and informal electronic sources.

I was a convert and instantly decided that I was going to implement the e-portfolio into one of the hospitality modules. However, I was adamant that my own lapse in engagement would not happen to the hospitality students at Queen Margaret University. Regular communication, activity and support at the beginning, middle and end were built into the programme and were critical for students to become fully engaged with the e-portfolio. Not only that, but I wanted to ensure the continuous use of the e-portfolio, so that by the time of the final assessment students were well equipped to design and attach an appropriate range of artefacts and discuss their learning journey since starting the module.

Creating an environment for students to practise reflection and the use of e-portfolio was critical to the students' success. Practice makes perfect and to this end, a number of guided learning sessions were arranged, along with practical tutorials and a structured learning guide for students to use throughout the module. Students were also encouraged, on a weekly basis, to discuss what was meant by reflection, and we had some exercises and practice sessions in tutorials.

Communication with students had to be clear from the outset, as they needed to be aware of what was required to succeed in the module. This was clarified during an informal induction which introduced students to the e-portfolio tool and discussed the importance of reflective learning. The session also included a demonstration on the different functions such as keeping and storing blogs, attaching a range of artefacts – photos, scanned graphics and journals that would help them develop and design their own e-portfolio. During the session students were provided with the details of fortnightly practical sessions which were to be delivered over a twelve week period. These sessions were to encourage students to engage with the process and help them to start thinking critically about what and how they were studying.

The induction session for the International Hospitality Management Programme and more specifically the *Food and Beverage Management Module* (2009) was also a good opportunity to introduce the course team but I also used induction to inform students of my own mistakes and demonstrate my own e-portfolio. I discussed my own mistakes and admitted that I did not get the best learning experience because I didn't attend the practical workshops. I declared that because I had left the design and submission of my assessment to the last minute, it was late in the day when I realised that it was not a simple task. My earlier lack of engagement, and hence knowledge, had made it extremely difficult to find my way around the e-portfolio system.

I encouraged students to practise as much as possible, because moving around the e-portfolio can be complicated and time consuming. It is better to build up experience gradually. I informed students that in hindsight, I was extremely frustrated and disappointed in myself for not building up practical skills with the technology. This declaration did overwhelm the students somewhat, but when I emphasised that we would be going through the process together, as a team, they seemed to relax and become quite enthusiastic about the challenge, particularly when I informed them that they were the first group in the business department to use this activity. I also reminded the students again of the guided learning sessions, practical tutorials and the structured learning guide to use throughout the module.

It was explained to the students that their portfolios should demonstrate what is important about an individual's learning at particular points in time. For instance, students should discuss and reflect on their learning and achievements, by asking themselves: did I do something exceptionally well, or could I have done something another way, or perhaps even better? The e-portfolio should be providing a rich and well-informed picture of an individual's abilities, aspirations and ambitions during the course of a module. This can be achieved by keeping weekly electronic blogs or diaries.

The aim of the e-portfolio is similar to its paper counterpart, as it is produced at key points in a learning journey. However, e-portfolios have many benefits, including the elimination of physical storage problems and accessibility. Furthermore, tutors can tap into the e-portfolio and it has the capability of allowing tutors to track students, aggregate and disaggregate data, and organise curricula around professional standards more easily than doing these tasks manually. This is of particular relevance to institutions with large numbers of students (Mayer & Latham, 2008)

Encouraging students to use blogs to host their weekly diaries and engage with the whole e-portfolio experience was fundamental to the development of their learning. Right from the start it was important that students engage with the e-portfolio to up date their diaries on a weekly basis. Practice helps students become more confident with the system, as well as inspiring ownership of e-portfolios. It creates friendly competition with students working and discussing how well their projects are developing. Practice also means that students are not frantically trying to put their e-portfolios together at the last minute and actually take the time to demonstrate reflection, evolution of thought, and professional development.

As mentioned, the e-portfolio software allows designated staff to enter a student's e-portfolio and check activity and performance. I checked up on students at various times throughout the weeks and sent electronic feedback via the e-portfolio. The e-portfolio is very flexible, not requiring tutors to be with students to check on performance or provide feedback.

Further, establishing respect for each other and for the leadership provided by the tutors was another essential part in establishing an effective e-portfolio environment and enabling the practice to work. Staff knowledge and training, an enthusiastic coordinator to start the process and maintain momentum through the various stages of implementation, are paramount to enhance the student learning experience and allow the activity to work.

Experienced staff who have been through this learning process can inspire trust because they know when to arrange additional sessions for students at various stages throughout the module. As mentioned, we held fortnightly practical sessions, which allowed me to check on student progress. I also implemented guided learning sessions in the middle and end of the module because I could help students who were not engaging. Furthermore, providing guidance at the end is just as important as the beginning and middle, as students need to learn how to submit their e-portfolio through the gateway.

Incidentally, the individual tasked with implementing the e-portfolio throughout the university was available every Friday for drop-in-sessions. Her valuable experience and patience was crucial to the success of the students; she has invited me to be an, 'e-portfolio ambassador' by demonstrating my students' work to other departments in the university. So, team work, a good induction process, clarity in what is expected from the students, clear time frames for additional sessions and communication are the key to getting students engaged and inspired to create their own e-portfolio and not think of it as additional work. Staff must provide consistent advice and guide the reflective process, and they must also make space in the timetable for guided learning sessions and practical tutorials.

Challenges and lessons learned

There were several challenges arising from the use of and implementing e-portfolio systems that might be of use to tutors intending to embark on the process. Firstly, adequate resources need to be made available to both staff and students which include guided learning sessions, practical tutorials and a structured learning guide. Staff and students need time to learn how to use the system with confidence. I found that designing my own e-portfolio was the best way for me to learn, even though I could have attended more practical classes to make my learning easier. Perhaps, tutors could use the e-portfolio to design their own PDP, thus becoming more familiar with the technology and gaining the skills to help guide their students through the learning. Alternatively, tutors could attend staff training, although I found practice was the easiest method.

Another challenge that became apparent at the beginning of the module was that students tended to write about their wonderful experiences rather than be reflective and honest. Early on, they were either writing to try and inform the tutor that they were not having any problems, or they did not fully understand what was meant by reflection. However, after we had continually discussed the key concept of reflection and ensured that students were clear in their understanding, they became more relaxed, less apprehensive and their work began to improve. In order to reinforce the approach we undertook a few practical examples throughout the module, so that students could get used to being reflective learners.

Probably the most significant feedback from students was that eventually the e-portfolio helped them to become reflective and openly identify and discuss their own learning, challenges and professional practice issues. However, to achieve success it is crucial that tutors have a clear idea of why they want to use e-portfolios and this must be clearly articulated to students. Tutors must also be prepared to invest some time in generating appropriate activities and also be prepared for it to take several attempts for students to understand the meaning of being a reflective learner and grasp the practicalities of using the e-portfolio. I found that showing students an example of an e-portfolio gave them an idea of what is expected of them and helped motivate them into creating something similar.

As previously mentioned, one of the most crucial aspects of enabling the e-portfolio to work was reflecting on my own learning experience. This helped me to be organised and ensure that I had appropriate systems in place to help students overcome their insecurities about the module. Nevertheless, it did become apparent in the first few weeks of using reflection and the e-portfolio system that students found the task quite daunting.

However, it was refreshing to discover that feedback from the second-year international hospitality students strongly supported the usefulness of the guided learning sessions, practical tutorials and a structured learning guide. It was even highlighted on module evaluation forms that one of the main areas of good practice was clear and continuous explanations on how to plan and develop the e-portfolio and the reflective process. Further, the majority of students reported that just having the opportunity to discuss the e-portfolio system with a tutor was most useful and provided a greater insight into the challenges and opportunities of the system. Evaluation forms also stated that, although students found the e-portfolio challenging, they also found it more valuable, interesting and engaging than any other assessment tool.

So, there was a significant amount of positive student feedback regarding the use of e-portfolio as a learning and teaching tool and it has been identified as an innovative type of assessment which has enhanced reflective processes. Granted students felt that it was quite a lot of work and quite a lot to learn, but they also found it challenging and most enjoyable. From my own perspective, it was extremely time-consuming organising the practical sessions and even more time-consuming ensuring that students were equipped with the correct tools in order to undertake the assessments. However, I have noticed a marked improvement in student work from previous years since using the e-portfolio as a reflective learning, teaching and assessment tool.

References

Corwin, T. (2003) Electronic Portfolios. *Campus-Wide Information Systems* 20 (1) p 32

Gray, L. (2008) *Effective Practice with e-Portfolios, Supporting 21st century learning*. Bristol: JISC

Mayer, B. & Latham, N. (2008) Implementing Electronic Portfolios: Benefits, Challenges, and Suggestions. *EDUCAUSE Quarterly* 31 p1

Nickelson D (2004) A computer-based approach to exploring science teachers' pedagogical content knowledge. *The Science Teacher* 71 (4) p 52

ISLE (2007) *ISLE: Individualised Support for Learning Through e-Portfolios*. Scottish Funding Council e-Learning Transformation Programme

Van Sickle, M., Bogan, M. B. & Kamen, M. (2005) Dilemmas faced establishing portfolio assessment of preservice teachers in the southeastern United States. *College Student Journal* 39 (3) p 497

Wetzel, K., & Strudler, N. (2005) The diffusion of electronic portfolios in teacher education, *College Student Journal* 39 (3) p 497

World Wide Web

Beetham, H (2005) e-Portfolios in post 16 learning in the UK: developments, issues and opportunities. At http://www.jisc.ac.uk/uploaded_documents/eportfolio_ped.doc (accessed 26/07/09)

Barrett, H. and J. Carney. (2005). Conflicting Paradigms and Competing Purposes in Electronic Portfolio Development. At http://electronicportfolios.com/portfolios/LEAJournal-BarrettCarney.pdf (accessed 12/07/06)

Ward, R. and Grant, S. (2007) 'An introductory paper- What is an e-portfolio?' *Centre for Recording Achievement* At http://www.recordingachievement.org/eportfolios/keydocs.asp (accessed 28/08/09).

PAULINE A. GORDON was Programme Leader of International Hospitality Management at Queen Margaret University in Edinburgh. Her academic interests include: investment appraisals in hospitality businesses and teaching, learning and assessment. She is currently lecturing at Edinburgh Napier University.

8

Using group-work assessment to encourage peer learning on a postgraduate programme

Sara Garratt
Canterbury Christ Church University

This chapter describes the development of a series of group-work assessments on a postgraduate business programme, recruiting a culturally diverse student body. The intention was to develop assessment practices that would fully engage students in team working and encourage them to value each other as sources of learning.

Introduction

The full time masters in business and management at Canterbury Christ Church University recruits predominately international students. As such, teaching staff are faced with many of the issues described elsewhere (amongst others, see De Vita, 2000). One particular concern for the staff teaching on this programme has been students' apparent reluctance to engage in, and consequently benefit from, group activities. Group work in various forms is central to many UK masters programmes. The Quality Assurance Agency for Higher Education cites 'effective performance within team environments...' as a skill that should be developed on all masters programmes (QAA, 2007: 7).

Canterbury Christ Church University, in common with many other UK universities has identified the ability to work effectively with others as a key component of the taught postgraduate curriculum. The development of this skill contributes to students' effectiveness both on the programme and in their subsequent working lives. For these reasons, great care has been taken by the programme team to build group work activities and assessments into the programme design in order to encourage the development of team working skills.

However, previous experience of the team has shown that students have been less enthusiastic about undertaking group work. Many students prefer to study independently, and appear frustrated by the added pressure of having to negotiate with a group. Others fear that their grades are likely to suffer or that they will have to put extra effort into the task and that their own contribution will not be fairly assessed. They do not seem put value on group work or value their peers as sources of learning, a central tenet of the ethos of group learning. In summary, contrary to the opinions of their tutors, students do not appear to believe that group work is a good way of learning (Wicaksono, 2008).

This lack of engagement seems to be exacerbated when one is working with a culturally diverse student group. Reynolds and Trehan (2009) have commented on the way differences are generally assumed to be a positive aspect of group work but reality is often experienced as a difficult and uncomfortable process. A lack of engagement in or unease with group work seems to be aggravated by cultural differences (Ledwith et al, 1998; Higgins & Li, 2009).

If students lack the skills or motivation to work effectively in groups (or are reluctant to work with each other), then the group learning strategy is not working as anticipated. After some reflection on students' general lack of enthusiasm for group work, I came to the conclusion that one way of making the intended learning process more effective might be through changing the assessment. When students are required to undertake a group assignment, the final mark is usually on the basis of the product – the work that the group submits. If a part of the mark is allocated to group processes then this is usually a small percentage of the total mark and is included to discourage the practice of 'free-riding' where a member of a group benefits by sharing the awarded grade but does little to contribute to the set task (see Pitt, 2000 for a good account of this).

I take the view that how students choose to learn is largely determined by how they are assessed (Parsons & Drew, 1996). By making the group process itself the focus of the assessment, I hoped to make group learning a more valuable experience for all concerned. I particularly wanted to design a series of activities that would encourage students to engage with group work and make it a valuable learning experience for them.

Context

The assessment relates to a 20-credit *Management and Leadership* module on the MSc business and management degree. The module consists of ten three-hour sessions over ten weeks. The assessment was a case study analysis (75%), individual participation in a series of set tasks and a reflective log where students were asked to reflect on their learning from these activities (25%). Seventeen students took this module. They came from Bangladesh, China, the Czech Republic, France, Libya, Slovakia, and the United Kingdom.

Description

The case study analysis was a formal written assignment. The rest of the assessment was in two parts:

a   an evaluation of each individual's participation in a series of activities that students engaged in over the course of the module

b   a reflective-learning log.

Students were set individual and group tasks each week. They were assessed on the completion of these tasks and the four tasks in which they scored the highest comprised their formal assessed mark. The reflective-learning log was written individually.

Group membership was allocated rather than self-selected for the group tasks and the groups changed each week. A group leader was appointed for each weekly group task. Each student had the opportunity to be a group leader at least once. Students were made aware that they would be assessed on their leadership and participation as much as on the quality of the completed task.

In the first session, the class discussed and drew up a list of the skills and competences they felt were important for effective management and leadership. These formed the basis of the tasks that were subsequently set.

The assessment

Students were set different individual and group tasks to complete each week.

Group tasks

Typically the group tasks consisted of a critical analysis of a case study, an investigation into and report on an issue, or research into and presentation of a management/ leadership skill. Examples included:

❑ How to make a sales pitch
❑ How to persuade a group to adopt an unpopular policy or decision
❑ How to negotiate

When the group had presented their completed task, the leader and the members were asked to report to the class on the group processes. They were given the following general prompts:

❑ Analyse the leadership style, what do you think went well?
❑ What difficulties did you feel you had to deal with?
❑ What would you do differently next time?

Individual and paired tasks

Each week students were given one or more tasks to complete, including directed reading in order to prepare for a class discussion, analysing small case studies, preparing a presentation, following some of the learning activities downloaded from the E-Evolve repository of learning materials (http://www.uclan.ac.uk/lbs/e-evolve/index. php) and putting the lessons learned into practice in class group activities.

Management briefings

One of the first tasks was for students to prepare and give 'management briefings' on business protocols in their own countries. This included accepted ways of giving critical feedback in these countries. The class was particularly interested in exploring and discussing the contrasting ways this was done in Slovakia, China and Libya.

This made us all much more culturally sensitive and self-aware in the later exercises when students gave feedback to each other.

E-Evolve

Good use was made of a range of resources from the E-Evolve Repository, a free resource bank of learning activities and materials that can be downloaded and made available to students in a virtual learning environment. (http://www.employability. org.uk/about). Students were required to access a series of resources and complete the learning activity, including examples such as Cross-cultural working, Practical impression management and Assertiveness. One of the most useful resources for the programme was 'How to give and receive feedback' which provided us with a good model we could use. My intention was to focus the students on developing their skills in giving feedback as much as receiving it. When a group presented their task, the class was asked to give feedback to the group and students were assessed on their ability to give constructive feedback.

Assessing the tasks

Students were individually assessed and participation in the set tasks was assessed by the tutor on the following basis:
❑ Did the student participate?
❑ Did the student participate reasonably effectively?
Students who participated fully and were judged by the tutor to have been effective would receive full marks for that task.

The reflective learning log

I wanted to encourage students to reflect on their experiences in conducting the tasks in order to stimulate self-awareness of their changing attitudes, skills, development and learning throughout the module. Students were required to reflect on four activities they had engaged in during the course. Suggested headings were:
❑ What did the task involve?
❑ What did I do well?
❑ What problems did I encounter?
❑ What did I learn from this activity?
❑ What would I do differently if I had the chance to do it again?
The Reflective Log was assessed on the criteria of the extent to which the log
❑ evaluated rather than simply described performance
❑ demonstrated the ability to identify one's strengths and weaknesses
❑ demonstrated the ability to plan for, manage and develop one's learning.

Evaluation

I feel the changes introduced in the assessment process did meet the objectives of encouraging active participation in learning and student engagement, developing students' team working skills; and encouraging students to value and learn from the diversity of nationalities present in the classroom. Students seemed much more engaged and ready to discuss and take an active part in all seminar activities, not just the set tasks. The group also mixed much more naturally and easily than they had done hitherto.

Feedback from students was generally very positive. Typical comments from students indicated they liked the practical application and development of skills:

> 'I really enjoyed the practical application of what we have been learning throughout the course.'

Several students said they felt more stress in this module, but this did not seem to be a negative observation:

> 'I felt pressure in this lesson but it made me study more effectively'.

Comments in the Reflective Log indicated that students had gained confidence in working in groups and had also increased their awareness of their own strengths and weaknesses both in group work and in team leading. Of course, some students continued to find working in groups uncomfortable, and not all students were fully engaged. But their colleagues seemed better able to develop strategies to deal with this. As one student commented in their Reflective Log:

> 'I have learnt that I have to accept the fact that there always will be people in the group who do not contribute to the task and they will disrupt the harmony in the group. I realised that dealing with this kind of person requires a lot of patience, there is still room for improvement and I need to work on it. At the end of the task I took a view that if there is nobody to stand behind the "weaker members", there is nothing wrong with taking action and helping them to feel involved.'

Other students reported that they had gained some good insights by working with such a diverse range of peers and the exercises did seem to break down some of the cultural barriers.

> 'I learned an important lesson in how different cultures can work together and how this can affect working relationships.'

> 'I used to work in a Chinese company. At that time, I always followed my manager without any personal ideas. However, I got a chance to lead my team in the class. Actually, this is my first time faced with how to manage team members. Although I felt it was different to deal with, I liked this job. I have learned the key skill for cross cultural communication which is 'take turns', it meant making a point and then listening to the response.'

> '(The) management and leadership module gave us more chance to talk about opinions by ourselves and practise as in real situations. (At first) everyone kept distance, Asian and European classmates sitting on different tables and same group members did every presentation..... through a series of tasks with different group members, everyone became more communicative and known to each other'

Discussion

In the revised assessment, I felt I was able to create a process by which students could develop and reflect on their management and leadership skills. I have always found this difficult to do when teaching students who have little or no practical experience of business and management.

Student involvement

Most students fully engaged with the process, but not all. Attempts to 'free-ride' still occurred, although other students seemed better able to challenge this by virtue of their formal role as team leader and/or through a genuine wish to develop their management and leadership skills.

One student who took on one of the first group leadership tasks described how the other members of the group put pressure on her to do the majority of the work and reduce all contact to email. However, she took her leadership role very seriously and insisted the group met several times, allocating different tasks to different people and demanding that they get involved.

'If I hadn't tried and managed to get involvement from my team the group analysis would have ended up being entirely my own work.'

The majority of other students took her lead in meeting the spirit of the assignments and conducting the work in face-to-face groups. But at least one appointed group leader did decide to lead from a distance:

'We did not meet together to discuss what we were doing. The team leader gave us our assignments which were issued by email... and then collected in the information to make the final assignment.'

From the group leader's perspective, the task was completed in an efficient manner. He did not have to spend his time or the time of the group with avoidable meetings, but the group members themselves seemed disappointed by his approach. They appeared offended that their group leader did not appear to see any particular value in working more closely with them.

'(the team leader) doesn't really talk to us outside the classroom. He just likes to be with his own friends'

I realised from reading their reflective logs that students in this group had used this experience to clarify their ideas about effective management and leadership behaviours; in this instance, that an important part of management and leadership is investing time in developing a relationship with the people you manage. Sometimes good learning comes from a poor experience.

Giving feedback

By focusing on developing skills of giving feedback and by using a clear framework for giving feedback, I had hoped to overcome the reluctance of students to criticise each other. We did have discussions about how negative feedback could be given in different countries and tried to role play this, but on the whole, politeness rather than directness won out:

'Most of the time we gave positive feedback avoiding the negative ones'

I felt the assessment was successful in encouraging students to value and learn from the diversity of nationalities present in the classroom. My impression was that students gained much more respect for each other and the majority realised how fortunate they were to be able to learn to work with different international groups and how this could impact favourably on their future careers.

We all gained useful insights into different cultural values and business practices which became a useful starting point for critically analysing management and leadership theory. All became more self aware and sensitive to cultural differences as this comment demonstrates:

'Unfortunately I was very late to one of the group meetings which is very common in my culture but (*which*) definitely upset them'

Lessons learned

❏ Attempts by group members to 'free-ride' or avoid active participation are likely to occur in the first tasks. It is important that group leaders in these early tasks are carefully chosen and are briefed actively to involve everyone from the start.

❏ It was very important to situate management and leadership in a multicultural context from the outset. So many texts on the subject take a purely western perspective with, perhaps, one chapter addressing 'culture'. Giving equal weight to effective leadership and management behaviours in very contrasting cultures was essential in making sure everyone felt they had an important contribution to make to activities and class discussions.

❏ I wanted students to reflect on the activities they had been involved in so a crucial element of the assessment design was the Reflective Log. I was worried that they would find this a difficult task but the standard of work submitted was very high. I realise that this was because students had been encouraged to reflect on their experiences each week in class discussions so the written reflective log was a natural extension of these discussions.

❏ It was important to formally structure the way students gave constructive critical feedback to each other. The E-Evolve resources provided a good basis for this but I underestimated how uncomfortable the prospect of giving critical feedback makes students feel. I might introduce more role play next time: asking students to role play giving critical feedback in different simulated situations.

❏ Basing the exercises on a list of the skills and competences that the students themselves had identified as important for effective management was a good idea. It helped them to connect what we were doing in the class with their future careers. I still underestimated how much students want to feel they are developing 'real life' leadership and management skills on business programmes. I might consider raising weighting of this assessment in the future.

Conclusion

I wanted to design a series of activities that would encourage a culturally diverse class of students to engage with group work and to make it a valuable learning experience for them. The activities were designed to develop a set of skills and competences that the students themselves had identified as bing important.

Group leaders and group membership were allocated on a changing weekly basis. Participation in and reflection on the set of activities was formally assessed. This encouraged student engagement and commitment to the module from the start. Students gained respect for each other and seemed to develop stronger relationships as a result.

The quality of work that students submitted in these activities was consistently excellent. Feedback on the activities was generally very positive: they seem to have realised that group work can be a good way of learning after all.

References and URLs

De Vita, G. (2000) Inclusive approaches to effective communication and active participation in the multicultural classroom: an international business management context. *Active Learning in Higher Education* 1 (2) pp. 168–80

E-Evolve Repository. Available from: (http://www.employability.org.uk/about) (last accessed 11 November, 2009)

Higgins, P. & Li, L. (2008) Fostering the appropriate learning environment? British and Chinese students' experiences of undertaking an organisational-based cross-cultural group workproject in a London university. *The International Journal of Management Education* 7 (3) pp. 57–67

Ledwith, S., Lee, A., Manfredi, S. & Wildish, C. (1998) *Multi-culturalism, student group work and assessment.* Oxford, England: Oxford Brookes University

QAA (2007) *Degrees in Business & Management 2007.* Available from: (http://search.qaa.ac.uk)

Parsons, D. E. & Drew, S. K. (1996) Designing group project work to enhance learning: key elements. *Teaching in Higher Education* 1 (1) pp. 65–80

Pitt, M. J. (2000) The Application of Games Theory to Group Project Assessment. *Teaching in Higher Education* 5 (2) pp. 233–41

Reynolds, M. and Trehan, K. (2009) Learning from Difference? *Management Learning* 34 (2) pp. 163–80

Wicaksono, R. (2008) Assessed mixed nationality group work at a UK university: does it get results? In R Atfield and P Kemp *Enhancing the International Learning Experience* Newbury UK: Threshold Press

SARA GARRATT is a principal lecturer at Canterbury Christ Church University and the Director of Postgraduate Programmes in the Faculty of Business and Management. Her main teaching areas are Leadership Studies and Research Methods. Her research interests are in the area of teaching and learning, with particular interests in assessment and in plagiarism.

9

Assessing work-related learning using e-portfolios

Ian Beattie
Liverpool John Moores University

The approaches and methods used to support and assess work-based learning need to be robust. With this in mind, this chapter studies the use of e-portfolios to assess Liverpool John Moores University Level 5 sport development students undergraduates undertaking a four-week placement.

Introduction

To be effective, work-based learning (WBL) must involve not only acquiring knowledge and skills related to the world of work, but also developing the meta-competence of 'learning to learn'. According to Lucas & Greany (2000: 5) 'learning to learn' is

> a process of discovery about learning. It involves a set of principles and skills which, if understood and used, help learners to learn more effectively and so become learners for life. At its heart is the belief that learning is learnable.

This statement comes from a schools context but learning for life is an important notion, and this meta-competence has an opportunity to flourish in setting personal learning goals for work-based learning. Accordingly, assessment of and support given to recognise evidence of this competence is vital. (Allin & Turnock, 2007). JISC states that

> the primary aim of an e-portfolio may be to collect evidence for summative assessment, to demonstrate achievement, record progress and set targets or to nurture a continuing process of personal development and reflective learning (2008: 6).

The e-portfolio has the potential to allow the student to collate, in one place, goals and evidence for personal learning and achievement of assessment criteria.

E-portfolios can be a valuable assessment tool (Lorenzo and Ittleson, 2005) and we must remember when enhancing assessment practice that 'there are important considerations ...' (JISC, 2007b: 8); certainly the approaches and methods used to support and assess WBL need to be robust.

Rationale

According to JISCinfoNET (2006) ideal assessment should be valid, reliable, practicable, fair, and useful to the student. It should demonstrate whether, and to what level, students have met the intended learning outcome(s) of the course, programme or module.

Increasingly, evidence indicates that well-planned and well-installed diagnostic and formative assessment can foster more effective learning for a wider diversity of learners (Nicol, 2006; Sharpe, Benfield, Roberts and Francis, 2006; JISC, 2007b). At the most fundamental level the rationale for developing e-portfolios in assessing WBL and subsequently work-related learning (WRL) is the need for improved assessment methods.

Students are assessed in three stages at Level 5 of the Sport Development programme. Through the completion of these stages, students must identify key areas for their development and in doing so must identify their individual learning requirements.

Stage 1

Pre-placement: the key question for students is 'What do I want to get out of this placement?' Before the end of Level 4 students must have completed the relevant paperwork and had a meeting with their personal tutor. At this tutorial, students discuss the paperwork (a learning agreement containing their learning objectives, a SWOT and a Skill analysis of themselves, a curriculum vitae and an action plan for their WBL placement).

Stage 2

During the placement: students are required, two weeks into placement, to e-mail their tutor with any adaptations and justifications for changes to their learning objectives/action plan. If no changes are to be made they must also justify this decision.

Stage 3

Post-placement: the students have to answer the question 'What did I get out of my placement?' They present an informal, concise summary (lasting five minutes) to answer this question for their tutor and tutor group.

Finally, to complete the portfolio, they must complete all the elements described above from Stage 1 demonstrating development, undertake a reflection of the WBL experience and produce an action plan to feed forward into their final year. When carrying out their reflection students are asked to consider the following questions:

❏   What have I done?
❏   What did I achieve?
❏   Where is the evidence?

The move to e-portfolios in this context came about for three reasons. First, there was an argument that conventional *portfolios* are just a collection of documents relating to learner progress, development and achievement and while it may be reasoned that an e-portfolio is just a similar collection of electronic documents, it is the connectivity and usability of the electronic portfolio that gives it added value (Beetham, 2005). The facility offered to students to interact with the collection of documents furthermore makes it distinctive. The second point is the reduction of paper waste. Thirdly, the move to electronic submission acknowledges that developed IT skills are an important graduate attribute.

The third and final point is important if one accepts that amongst the key education challenges for the UK is the need to develop a more highly skilled workforce to compete in an increasingly competitive global market (Leitch, 2006). This issue is just as relevant in today's economic climate as it was when first published and that is unlikely to change.

Liverpool John Moores University context

JISC contend that introducing e-assessment can enhance the quality of the learner's experience when it is developed alongside the pedagogic approach used, and indeed that 'e-Assessment can play a significant part in a more flexible and personalised environment for learning...' (2007b: 10)

The robust assessment of WBL and WRL, along with a student-centred approach to learning, are integral to the programmes delivered by the sport team in the Centre for Sport, Dance and Outdoor Education at Liverpool John Moores University (LJMU); their added value and importance are embedded in the ethos of the centre staff. This philosophy has been implicitly and explicitly developed since the programme's inception in 1999 and in subsequent programme reviews and validations. The enhancement of learning, teaching and assessment is the focal point for each member of staff, through staff-development days, planning days or awaydays.

Furthermore, the ability to capture and demonstrate 'a set of achievements...that make graduates more likely to gain employment and be successful in their chosen occupations, which benefits themselves, the workforce, the community and the economy' (Yorke & Knight, 2006: 3) while not the exclusive rationale for developing e-assessment, lent weight to the argument for it.

Employability is introduced and explained to students in their programme and module handbooks, in personal tutor sessions and through personal development planning (PDP) at all levels of the programme. This process begins as soon as the students start Level 4. Even before joining the university, potential students are made aware of the importance of employability in the programme and the university. At interview days, the admissions officer welcomes the candidates to the proceedings and gives an overview of the institution, the programme of study, of WBL and WRL during their undergraduate studies and the importance of preparing themselves effectively as graduates to enter the world of work.

The Centre for Excellence in Teaching and Learning (CETL) in Leadership and Professional Learning is hosted at LJMU and the programme team subscribe to and advocate the overarching aim of the CETL. This is to develop existing innovative approaches to WRL and in doing so, to enhance students' vocational, leadership and entrepreneurial skills.

The sport development programme has work-based and related learning at all levels with a current intake of 100 students into Level 4 of the programme. PDP is an integral component and the students undertake a year-long PDP module at Level 4 which leads into PDP throughout Levels 5, 6 and beyond. The PDP module at Level 4 includes assessment tasks which require the students to create a personal website and an e-portfolio.

Over the years the team have used a variety of resources to support or assess students while they are on placement, as a part of PDP and through the work-related elements of the programme. These include Blackboard discussion boards, the Blog tool in Blackboard, e-portfolios and Facebook.

The use of e-learning resources in the sport portfolio in the Centre for Sport, Dance and Outdoor Education at LJMU had humble beginnings in 2004 with a group of nine Level 5 students using the discussion boards during their placement. This led to the integration of a variety of methods into learning, teaching and assessment (LTA) as a consequence of institutional policy and guidelines (such as the 'Blue Book' – LJMU's guide to effective assessment practice, LJMU Plus – the university's initiative to add value to the student experience and the LTA Strategy and implementation guide). The programme team continually review the relevance and currency of the programme in annual monitoring reviews, the feedback from National Student Surveys or in informal debates. The developments across the CETL have also led to numerous initiatives and new practices. All of these are driven by a focus on student employability.

After receiving a Teaching and Learning award in 2008, a project was implemented to develop an e-portfolio for a pilot group of Level 5 WBL students. This was a part of a bigger scoping exercise looking at the development of continuity in the use and application of a variety of e-learning resources across the cohort. The use of e-portfolios to assess Level 5 WBL became a key driver, and led to the inclusion of the WBL module in a university-wide project on the online submission of coursework.

The e-portfolio is an attractive means of assessing WBL because it can be used 'to collect evidence for summative assessment, to demonstrate achievement, record progress and set targets' or 'to nurture a continuing process of personal development and reflective learning'. (JISC, 2008: 6). For the purposes of the WBL module, we decided that both these options were relevant, in keeping with the range of purposes that e-portfolios might serve across a lifetime of learning (JISC, 2007a). Remember, the meta-competence of 'learning to learn' is important in achieving effective work-based learning and PDP activities, from Level 4 through to WRL in Level 6 and beyond, lend themselves easily to adopting and embracing e-portfolios.

We evaluated a number of e-learning resources and found that they were effective and useful for undertaking, reflecting upon and evidencing personal learning and development established via WBL at Level 5. PDP is not the sole property of WRL – students undertake PDP across all levels – partly, this follows from work carried out by the team to embed PDP and partly from institution-level requirements for PDP.

While we acknowledge that the 'variety of applications of e-assessment reported and their innovation and general effectiveness indicate the potential of e-assessment ... and the ability for e-assessment ...to significantly enhance the learning environment and the outcomes for students...' (Open University, 2006: 4), it is crucial to be aware that embracing e-learning could lead to information overload. It was felt that resources had been used largely on an ad hoc basis; so this project aimed at a systematic approach to the use of e-learning across the sport portfolio. By developing a framework for Level 5 WBL assessment and linking this to other levels and modules, we hoped to achieve consistency and provide clarity for the students.

What is the activity/practice trying to achieve and why?

Through this practice we aim to provide an effective means for the auditing and evidencing of graduate skills. In the past, students have presented their WBL portfolios in a paper-based file which, at best, allowed them to provide creative evidence (by using supporting appendices) on their placement but, at worst, required a forklift truck to collect the work for marking.

WBL assessment requires reflection, and this is enhanced by the effective use of e-learning resources. The ability to hyperlink to provide evidence, external links and audio or video clips to support the reflections required in assessing WBL, all offer students the opportunity to develop efficient and coherent e-portfolios.

What are the main features of the approach taken?

While the use of Blackboard to provide ways and means of assessment of WBL and WRL has been developed in a variety ways at LJMU, the e-portfolio for Level 5 WBL is the focus of this chapter.

The Level 5 WBL e-portfolio was built on a framework designed following the pilot project with the Level 5 group in 2008. The framework was designed to enable the students to develop their e-portfolio of evidence for the WBL module undertaken at the start of Level 5. The module requires students to carry out a minimum of 20 days in a placement of their choice and is assessed through three explicit stages, with tasks undertaken at each stage as shown in Figure 1. The move from Stage 1 to 3 allows the students to reach a point where reflection on their practice is supported by the evidence they collect at each stage.

By using the process diagram illustrated in Figure 1 we designed a framework of templates to allow students to create and develop their e-portfolio using the three stages. Additionally, blank templates were created for the various elements of required paperwork. These templates were developed as a part of the pilot project and were subsequently further amended for the following academic year. Before the submission of e-portfolios, copies of paperwork were made available as Microsoft Word documents and added to the module content folder in Blackboard along with the module handbook. These Word documents are still included and give the students the choice to use the templates designed in the e-portfolio or use the Word documentation in creating and developing their own e-portfolio.

When the students return to university on completing their WBL, they attend a lecture about developing their e-portfolio in Blackboard and then use the dedicated tutorial support given through the tutor system. It is in the first of these tutorials that students begin the process of completing Stage 3 by presenting an informal overview

Figure 1 – The process of completing the WBL section of your PDP portfolio

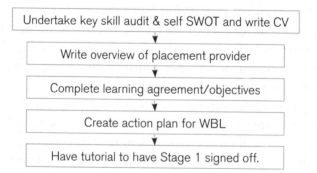

STAGE 1

Consider – "What do I want to get out of this placement?"

Undertake key skill audit & self SWOT and write CV

Write overview of placement provider

Complete learning agreement/objectives

Create action plan for WBL

Have tutorial to have Stage 1 signed off.

STAGE 2

Send e-mail to Tutor at midway point. Include amended Action Plan (if applicable) and justifications for choices made. You must justify why you have or have not amended your plan.

STAGE 3

Ask yourself – "What did I get out of my placement?"

Deliver 5 minute presentation to tutor & group

Update paperwork from Stage 1

Complete reflection of WBL experience

Create Action Plan for Level 3

Finally build relevant section (including appendices) in **PDP Portfolio**.

of their WBL to their tutor and peer group. Discussions take place at this point about the development of their e-portfolios and tutor support is available students prior to the submission of their work as it is for other assessment tasks.

On completing their e-portfolios, students share their work with the module leader and their tutor; this enables moderation to take place and it also enables the external examiners to be able to view and comment on the e-portfolios easily and efficiently.

How effective and appropriate are the e-portfolios?

Evidence to date is encouraging. The student feedback from the pilot group was positive. Responses to 'What did you like about the e-portfolio?' ranged from

> the e-portfolio is neater and tidier and allows for further development of ICT skills

to

> liked the outline of the whole thing, the colours and so on...it makes it look very professional.

When asked what they disliked about using the e-portfolio, one student commented that

> Uploading data and media was frustrating at times as it didn't always work. It did take a while to get used to and make sure that everything was appearing when I opened the e-portfolio.

However, students who made broadly similar points to these consistently added: '...but other than that I had no problems'. Every student stated they would use the e-portfolio again and all the pilot group are using an e-portfolio within Level 6 modules where it is appropriate.

Marks for those using the e-portfolio in this module were very good in comparison to those submitting paper-based versions (on average 80% as opposed to 60%) although as the pilot project consisted of less than 20% of the overall cohort, we should avoid reading too much into this. The portfolio (in either of the formats) was worth 100% of the module mark and the completion of the three stages and required number of days are the prerequisite for the portfolio. Students are given a module-specific handbook which offers guidance on these requirements, and the tutor support system allows discussions and negotiation to take place to ensure that the learning outcomes of the module are met. While caution is advised, the average mark and standard of work alongside the comments of the students was heartening.

The entire pilot group used e-portfolios in other modules to provide evidence of practice and they said anecdotally that the e-portfolio framework for WBL gave them more confidence in approaching and using other e-portfolios. E-portfolios were not new to the cohort but the framework for assessment of WBL was, and all the initial signs are encouraging. The students embraced e-portfolios as a valid way of evidencing their knowledge, skills and understanding across a variety of modules. The students from the cohort who used the e-portfolios have become advocates for adopting this method to provide evidence for assessment in other modules.

Two Level 6 students who had used e-portfolios the previous year assisted in the work undertaken with the Level 5 pilot group. They provided support to the students during pre- and post-WBL sessions. Their input was invaluable. It should be noted that the staff from the Learning Development Unit (LDU) and CETL ICT staff at I. M. Marsh Campus provided support to students and created the initial templates which mirrored stages one through to three, as seen in the process model in Figure 1.

There are two other points to acknowledge here. First, the development of these innovative approaches to assessment required investment, be that of staff or financial resources. Secondly, through engaging the students in the process of developing the assessment method they acquired a sense of ownership which led to wider adoption by the students of the programme.

A further point to consider when analysing the appropriateness of the e-portfolio in assessing the students can be seen in the standard of reflection in the e-portfolios. The evidence provided to support the e-portfolios was also very good and demonstrated the usefulness of the e-portfolio to hyperlink and be interactive. Figure 2 shows a screenshot from one e-portfolio to illustrate this.

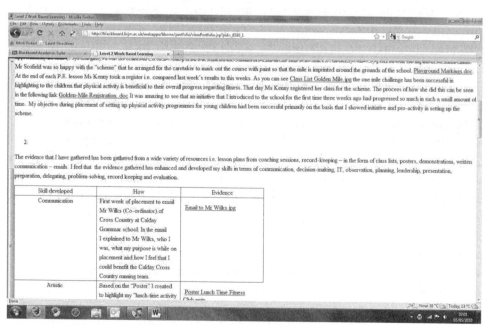

Figure 2 e-portfolio screenshot

There was also an unexpected outcome for academic staff relating to the marking of the e-portfolio: it was an easier process than before. Consequently, the decision was taken that all Level 5 students would, in future, submit their work in this form. A final point of note is that the Level 5 cohort for academic year 2009–10 achieved

61% average for the module with 20% of the students achieving a mark above 70%.

What enabled the practice to work and what lessons were learned?

The pilot group of Level 5 students consisted of nine students from one tutor group and a further five students joined the initial group. When asked why they wanted to submit an e-portfolio, all the additional students said that they had seen how the pilot group were progressing with their e-portfolios and they wanted to do the same. As one student commented, having seen his housemates developing their e-portfolios, 'I realise that the evidence I have collected can be presented much more effectively in an e-portfolio'.

Above all, it was the drive and focus of this group of students, in allowing the examination and exploration of the templates and framework in the pilot project, which enabled the project to work. This allowed the 2009–10 Level 5 cohort to use the e-portfolio to submit their assessment task for WBL.

The barriers and challenges faced were, as always, time constraints and occasionally there were technological errors (although these were quickly remedied with support from colleagues).

We would strongly recommend that colleagues interested in this approach embrace the potential of e-portfolios, perhaps initially for work-based learning if not for PDP as a whole.

❑ Don't be afraid of the technology.
❑ Innovative practice is not without its challenges but in embracing these encounters there can be interesting rewards.
❑ Encourage the students to be creative by keeping in mind the meta-competence of 'learning to learn'.
❑ Lead them to explore the boundaries beyond which that sought-after independent learner might appear.
❑ Finally, use other students to support students where appropriate.

References

Allin, L. and Turnock, C. (2007) Assessing Student Performance in Work-Based Learning. Available online at http://www.practicebasedlearning.org/resources/materials/docs/

Beetham, H. (2005) e-Portfolios in post-16 learning in the UK: developments, issues and opportunities. Available online at http://www.jisc.ac.uk/media/documents/themes/elearning/eportfolioped.pdf

JISC (2007a) e-Portfolios: an overview of JISC Activities, (first published in 2006). Available online at http://www.jisc.ac.uk/media/documents/publications/eportfoliooverview2006.pdf

JISC (2007b) Effective Practice with e-Assessment. An overview of technologies, policies and practice in further and higher education. Available online at http://www.jisc.ac.uk/media/documents/themes/elearning/effpraceassess.pdf

JISC (2008) Effective practice with e-Portfolios: supporting 21st century learning. Available online at http://www.jisc.ac.uk/media/documents/publications/effectivepracticeeportfolios.pdf

JISCinfoNET (2006) Characteristics of a 'Good' Assessment Programme. Available online at http://www.jiscinfonet.ac.uk/InfoKits/effective-use-of-VLEs/e-assessment/assess-characteristics/view

Leitch Review (2006) Prosperity for all in the global economy – world class skills. London: HMSO

Lorenzo, G. and Ittelson, J. (2005) An overview of e-portfolios. Educause. Available online at http://net.educause.edu/ir/library/pdf/ELI3001.pdf

Lucas, B. and Greany, T. (2000) (Eds) Learning to learn: setting the agenda for schools in the 21st century. London: Campaign for Learning

Nicol, D. J. (2006) Increasing success in first year courses: assessment re-design, self-regulation and learning technologies. Available online at www.ascilite.org.au/conferences/sydney06/proceeding/onlineIndex.html

Open University (2006) Roadmap for e-Assessment. Report for JISC. Available online at http://www.jisc.ac.uk/elp_assessment.html

Sharpe, R., Benfield, G., Roberts, G. and Francis, R. (2006) The undergraduate experience of blended e-learning: a review of UK literature and practice undertaken for the Higher Education Academy. Available online at: www.heacademy.ac.uk/4884.htm

Yorke, M. and Knight, P. (Reprinted 2006) Embedding employability into the curriculum. York: Higher Education Academy.

IAN BEATTIE is a Programme Coordinator for Sport Development at Liverpool John Moores University. He is a year tutor, work-related learning coordinator and the creator of a management group made up of industry professionals and academic colleagues brought together to enhance the curriculum. Before taking up his post at Liverpool John Moores University, Ian worked in the health and sports management industry for over 12 years in both the public and private sector, and was Club Coach for MerseyTri triathlon club.

Ian is an alumnus of the BA (Hons) Sport Development with PE course, and is currently undertaking an MSc in Sociology of Sport and Exercise. He has research interests in the use of sport development processes and initiatives within private/public sector leisure/sport and health provision and also management processes and their use within health, fitness and sport. Ian is the chair of the North West Health and Physical Activity Forum and a member of the Wirral Physical Activity Board.

Thanks must go to the staff from the Learning Development Unit who supported the building of the e-portfolio templates and framework, along with the CETL ICT staff, and to colleagues in the Centre.

10

'So when is the final exam, then?'
New forms of assessment and student engagement

Graham Baker
University of the West of England

This case study reflects on the introduction of a new programme of assessment on a Level 4 module for over 1,000 students in a large business school. The changes are part of a work in progress, were not introduced as a research intervention and, as such, have not been formally evaluated. The changes are described followed by a discussion of some of the key issues that arose.

Introduction

The chapter focuses on the practitioner level and describes how changes in assessment strategies are both possible on a very large module and also can lead to a better student experience; in particular how they can provide some valuable early formative feedback to students in preparation for their examinations.

Objectives

The aim of the change was to overcome some of the issues that had been identified with assessment following the introduction of the Graduate Development Programme (GDP) into the *Management and Organisational Behaviour* (MOB) module at Level 4 in the business school. This programme aims to develop the skills of graduates and at level 4 was focused on group work and academic skills (Baker and French, 2009). The main objectives of the assessment changes were to spread the assessment burden throughout the whole 22 weeks of the module and, in particular, to create an opportunity for different types of assessment experiences, to allow for the introduction of a research activity and to allow students to gain from some meaningful formative feedback early on in their first semester.

Rationale

The changes were introduced because it was felt that the students were being disadvantaged by the traditional assessment model. The following were key concerns:

❑ Students were used to a more regular assessment process and more regular feedback from staff than we were able to offer on this module. This perceived lack of formative feedback can be a factor in student disengagement. Baker (2006) argues that the anxiety caused by the transition into higher education increases the need for students to receive feedback on their progress from all sources. Students were excited and engaged at the start of the module but we risked losing these positive feelings as we had no provision for meaningful feedback during the first semester of the module.

❑ Trying to develop students as critical and self-reflective learners through the GDP was difficult in this situation. Students need to be able to find out how they were doing as they progressed through what Baker describes as 'studenthood' (2006: 172). At the same they needed to develop a range of skills, such as referencing or research based skills, which were not being developed in the traditional module format.

❑ The student body on the module was highly differentiated covering a wide range of programmes of study, social and ethnic backgrounds and learning experiences. As Race (2001) suggests, student diversity requires diversity in assessment.

❑ The traditional assessment programme placed a large burden on both students and staff over a relatively short period of time. To lighten this load there was a clear need to spread it over the whole year.

Context

The Management and Organisational Behaviour (MOB) module is delivered by staff in the organisation studies department. It is an introductory course which considers how people and organisations interact. It represents a core module in all the programmes offered by the business school with the exception of a small number of joint honours students. MOB also forms a core module in the management courses at a large affiliated institution in Gloucestershire and at a higher education institution in Malaysia. The module has nearly 1,100 students and 16 staff on the main campus and about 300 on the other sites, with four staff.

In 2007, the university introduced the GDP as a compulsory element for first year students. The GDP is a university-wide common approach to student learning and experience that aims to develop a distinctive 'UWE graduate'. It focuses on learning skills, personal development, employability and academic achievement. Level 4 students focus on the development of the skills and attitudes needed to be successful in higher education such as learning styles, academic writing and working in groups. The business school's approach to implementing this initiative was to embed the delivery of GDP within the MOB module.

Description

Until September 2008, MOB had taken a traditional approach to assessment with variations on an assignment and/or learning journal usually submitted in March, and a final examination in the May assessment period. The weighting was heavily in favour of the exam which contributed between 60% and 70% of the assessment. The consequences of this were:

❑ The students were not formally assessed until almost the end of the second half of the academic year and thus had no means of monitoring their progress until almost the end of the module.

❑ The scale of the module and the demands of standardising and moderating meant that feedback on written work, which was full and constructive, could only be available four teaching weeks later.

❑ In addition, the timing of assessment was often determined by the need to take advantage of the university non-teaching weeks to give staff longer to mark the work. This could extend the feedback to six or seven weeks later.

❑ There was no obvious formative assessment allowing feedback on progress and the end loading of assessment might have a negative impact on engagement as students were unable to gauge whether they were successful on the course or not.

❑ More instrumental students would focus on the assessment in semester two and might undervalue the course during semester one.

From September 2008 the assessment policy was changed to include six separate yet linked activities, as follows:

❑ Two short writing tasks of 500 words (Race, 2008) were introduced in the first semester after four and eight weeks with the aim of students seeing the 'assessment culture' (Race, 2001). Each was worth five per cent of the total assessment and was designed to give feedback on progress and to prepare students for the January exam – a key aim of formative feedback (Juwah at al, 2004) – by using the exam criteria as the basis for the feedback. The first assessment was handed in as students entered the lecture theatre in week four and feedback was given within about ten minutes of the start of the lecture. The students assessed their own work and the lecturer gave guidance as to the impact and importance of what they had or had not done. The assignment was read by their tutors and a comment made in time for the seminar the following week. The second assessment was peer-assessed in seminars and students could expect two or three sets of feedback within the seminar time.

❑ These two short assessments formed the basis of personal interviews undertaken in week 11 by seminar tutors. Students were expected to bring a completed 'feed forward' sheet to the interview which acted as a review document of what the feedback meant to them and, more importantly, how they intended to use the feedback in their future learning both in this subject and across other modules (Gibbs and Simpson, 2002). The aim was to try and ensure the students were clear about the demands of the examination.

❑ The exam was moved to January from the traditional May assessment period and the marks were reduced to 30% of the total assessment for the module.

❏ A learning journal was submitted in mid February, worth 20% of the total assessment. This covered many of the GDP areas and some MOB topics, including referencing exercises, self-reflection on learning styles and self motivation.

❏ A six-week group project on any relevant MOB topic, worth 20% of the total assessment, acted as a research activity, aimed at developing graduate attributes (Land and Gordon, 2008) and was assessed by a group presentation in the last two weeks of semester two.

❏ An individual assignment worth 20% of the total, based on theorising the experience of the group activity, was submitted at the beginning of the May assessment period.

Evaluation

The changes were not systematically evaluated as the project is a work-in-progress designed as a fundamental change to the structure of assessment rather than as an experiment. However, experience of certain aspects has led to some minor detail review for the academic year starting in 2009. These include focusing the group research project onto two topics, identifying ways in which the group aspect of the project can be assessed to create engagement over the last month of semester two and replacing the learning journal with a GDP activities portfolio.

Approximately 100 more students sat the exam in January than those following the traditional assessment schedule with the exam in May. This was felt to be a much better sign of engagement with the module. Unfortunately, more students failed the January exam than the 2007 May exam; perhaps because they were not mentally ready for an exam in the first twelve weeks of the module or thought it was not as important as it was. Overall the module pass rate fell following the first run of the module (before the referral exams). Yet more people gained a 40%+ mark for the module (83% in the 2008 academic year compared to 80% in the 2007). Whether this was a cohort or module issue was difficult to assess as MOB was the only module that had a written exam paper at the January assessment and so no comparison with other large modules could be made.

Student satisfaction given in the module feedback remained excellent. However, detailed feedback was inconclusive as the short feedback courseworks in the first semester received both praise and criticism from students.

The students seemed more engaged as a body with the group research project and the assignment which followed than they had been in the past with just an assignment. Students submitted a range of research projects and staff identified some very good attempts to engage with this research activity, and some excellent presentations. Tutors reported that students were clearly engaged in the subject far more than in the past as the need to research and think about the topics required a much longer period of focus than in previous years.

Although there were now more assessment points in the year, there was no criticism from students or staff about being over-assessed. Some students are used to more regular forms of assessment in their school or college experience anyway. Those students who were adult returners seemed to like the gentle easing in to assignment writing that the programme allowed. Staff spent less time marking throughout the year as many of the assessments were streamlined or done in class, helping considerably to balance the workload.

Discussion

A number of issues arose from the new assessment programme. Highly unexpectedly, some students were unprepared for the exam even though they were told about it regularly and the assessments were focused at preparing them for the demands of the exam. Discussions after the exam with students who had done badly suggested that they just did not realise how difficult the exam was going to be. Despite the existence of a mock paper with examples of the style of question they could expect they did not practise and were not prepared. So why was this?

❑ Some students who have already disengaged from the module see there is an exam, sit it and fail.

❑ Some students still expect an end of year exam despite all that has been said to them in lectures. They think either there will another chance, or that they will make up for any poor performance in the later exam. This is clearly linked in with a perception and a presumption amongst those that have taken A levels that they will be able to improve their results by re-sitting in the future. The end-of-year exam model is ingrained in to the psyche of students and of course, ingrained into the university assessment regulations, which make the default assumption of an end-of-year exam.

❑ There is a risk in being different from other modules in your assessment programme. As no other modules were setting written exams early, many students assumed that ours were unimportant or easy, despite the provision of a sample paper.

It is difficult being different. In our experience, students like the familiar, fear the unusual, and often see anything unexpected as threatening rather than as an opportunity to develop new skills or have new experiences.

Linked to the last point, is the issue of how students see self- and peer- assessment. In the eyes of some students only an assessment marked or read by a member of staff carries any worth, and this appeared in module feedback. Others relish the idea of peer assessment and enjoy seeing what other people have written as this allows them to gain a sense of how they are doing and receive feedback from a range of different people. Mature students did comment on the benefits of receiving feedback early on in their programmes before the 'important' assessments started.

There is a need to explain to students not only what type of assessment will take place but why they are being assessed in the way that they are. If they understand the rationale behind why they have to do different assessments, then they are far more willing to accept their validity as assessment. In the first run through of the new assessment strategy the explanation of the rationale was given at the beginning of the lecture during which they received their first feedback. With the latest run of the module the whole assessment strategy is explained in more depth and is closely aligned with the learning theory looked at in the 'learning in higher education' topic of the module.

The attempt to create more space for engagement across the whole module and reduce student instrumentality does paradoxically create more opportunities for students to behave instrumentally. The coursework element of assessment was broken down into five different activities. Those students who are liable to act instrumentally could decide to opt out of some of the later activities if they thought they had already passed the module before the final activity. If students do not complete all elements of the coursework, this has implications for funding, according to the Higher Education Funding Council for England's definition of module completion and the importance of the final assignment, which came out after the start of the semester (HEFCE, 2009). For most modules this is a final exam and is often the most important part of the assessment programme. But for MOB the final assessment is a piece of coursework only worth 20% of the total assessment; thus there could be funding implications if students were to decide that they had passed the coursework element before the hand-in date.

However, there was little evidence of this as those students who failed to hand in the final assignment tended to have not engaged with any of the coursework. In addition, the timings of the final coursework were determined to ensure that results were not known before the submission of the final two pieces.

Lessons learned and conclusion

In our experience, we would highlight six key points to consider when developing opportunities for adding formative feedback:

❑ Introduce small pieces of work which are easy to mark and which allow for quick feedback. Large student numbers and big modules make anything else difficult to manage and return within a short time.

❑ Make the activities relevant to other larger pieces of assessment – in this case the exam – so that the relevance of the feedback can be seen immediately.

❑ Make some marks available for these activities as an incentive for students to engage with formative feedback assignments. The aim is to make the process worth something without making it so important that anxiety levels rise. Give the marks for the production of the work and for engaging with the exercise rather than for the quality of the work – hence the small proportion of the total assessment mark. If marks are given for quality students tends to focus on the mark rather than the feedback and there could be moderation issues. A poor piece of work which provides the student with clear and rapid formative feedback can be a very powerful and positive learning experience, especially when it does not cause them to fail the coursework element of the module.

❏ Try self- and peer-assessment as means of developing immediate feedback rather than formal feedback.

❏ Inform students that the value and importance of feedback is more than the mark and that the most important aspect of feedback is what they do with it, not the feedback itself. Some students know what to do with feedback but many do not and thus continue making the same mistakes. There needs to be some mechanism by which the students can reflect on what they have learned from the exercise.

❏ Explain to students that there are more ways to show what they know about a subject than by testing them with an exam. Of course, examinations still play an important role in the assessment of the module and are a requirement to meet the regulatory demands for controlled-conditions assessment. Clearly explain the assessment rationale for the module and show how the January exam is used to test the students' understanding of two topics in semester one, rather than the whole course. The later assessments are designed to test research, presentation skills and writing skills but above all they are aiming to see if the students are developing the ability to see and think like successful students of organisation studies.

In conclusion, assessment can improve the student experience and encourage greater engagement. Assessment needs to be tailored not only to the demands of the course but also the needs of the students. As the nature of the student body changes so should the assessment that they have to undertake.

References and URLs

Baker, A. (2006) What else do students need? A psychodynamic reflection on students' need for support from staff at university. *Active Learning in Higher Education* 7 171–83

Baker, G. and French, R. (2009) Enhancing Student Learning. Managing tensions in a large undergraduate module. In Buswell, John and Becket, Nina *Enhancing Student-centred Learning in Business and Management, Hospitality, Leisure, Sport and Tourism.* Newbury UK: Threshold Press

Gibbs, G. and Simpson, C. (2002) *Does your assessment support your students' learning.* Available from http://www.open.ac.uk/fast/ Centre of Higher Education Practice: Open University

Higher Education Funding Council for England (2009) *Higher Education Students Statistics Survey 2009-10* [online]. Available from http://www.hefce.ac.uk/pubs/hefce/2009/09_36/ Accessed 17/3/2010

Juwah, C., Macfarlane-Dick, D., Matthew, B., Nicol, D., Ross, D. & Smith, B. (2004) *Enhancing student learning through effective formative feedback.* York: The Higher Education Academy (generic centre)

Land, R. and Gordon, G. (2008) *Research-Teaching Linkages. Enhancing Graduate Attributes. Sector Wide Discussions Vol 1.* Quality Assurance Agency for Higher Education. Available from www.enhancementthemes.ac.uk accessed 12/5/2009

Race, P. (2001) *A Briefing on Self, Peer and Group Assessment. Assessment Series 9.* York: Learning and Teaching Support Network Generic Centre.

Race, P. (2008) Assessment Seminar. Bristol Business School Teaching and Learning Training Day. Bristol

GRAHAM BAKER is a senior lecturer in the Department of Organisation Studies in the Bristol Business School, University of the West of England. He is the module leader of the Level 4 module Management and Organisational Behaviour and also leads a Level 6 module in Organisational Leadership. His main areas of research are learning and teaching, and power and resistance in organisations. Before joining the university, he spent eighteen years teaching at a senior level in a variety of secondary schools.

11

Assessment to enhance student learning in sport-related research

Rich Neil, Kylie Wilson and Richard Tong
Cardiff School of Sport, UWIC

This chapter describes how the authors revised the *Research Methods* module assessment strategy and feedback process at Cardiff School of Sport. The assessment strategy was to better reflect the content and delivery of the revised *Research Methods* module, while the feedback was targeted on specific criteria and individualised for each student.

Introduction

The key objectives of the Cardiff School of Sport strategic plan are to design and deliver high quality, research-informed, undergraduate and postgraduate sports-related courses in first class facilities, to foster a strong research culture, and to develop learning-orientated assessment that better supports learning. This case study presents the outcomes of a review to make the assessment strategy and feedback processes for a Level 4 *Research Methods* module more consistent with the school strategic plan. Before the review, the *Research Methods* module was focused on research outcomes (i.e. data analysis), consisted solely of lectures delivered to large groups (n=200) and was assessed at the end of the year by an examination.

Indeed, initial focus groups with Level 5 and Level 6 students who had previously taken the module and with current staff suggested that the Level 4 and 5 *Research Methods* modules did not challenge the students, were didactic in delivery style and used a poor assessment strategy. Consequently, many students had not engaged sufficiently or gained enough knowledge to produce an adequate research proposal at Level 5 or undertake an independent project at Level 6.

Revised assessment strategy

In an effort to make the *Research Methods* modules more consistent with the school strategic plan, we worked on redeveloping them at both levels to improve student learning about the research process. This case study will focus on the Level 4 module only. We aim to provide students with experiential learning of the research process, focusing on identifying issues and specific questions related to appropriate methods within each of the main disciplines in sport studies:

- ❏ sport biomechanics
- ❏ sport physiology
- ❏ sport and exercise psychology
- ❏ sport coaching
- ❏ sport development
- ❏ sport coaching
- ❏ sport management
- ❏ socio-cultural studies
- ❏ performance analysis.

Students then progress and work through the entire research process – including data analysis, interpretation and dissemination in Level 5 to prepare them for conducting dissertation at Level 6.

Teaching

Around 110 students were taught in four repeat lectures (total 440) and within each lecture they were guided through the research process in smaller groups of ten. Students worked through the process within all of the disciplines mentioned above in two-week blocks throughout the academic year. We then attempted to facilitate learning by using assessment strategies consistent with the structure of delivery and which addressed the learning outcomes of the module.

As students worked to identify the issues, formulate more specific questions by reading relevant literature, select appropriate methods and consider ethical dimensions, they were required to write an essay covering this process in week 14 (of a 24-week academic year). This fits alongside a formative assessment which they took at week 22 and a multiple-choice exam at the end of the year.[1] This assessment strategy differed from the previous academic year where only an end of year exam was conducted.

Feedback process

Students had to submit the essay as a paper copy and additionally electronically, through the internet-based Turnitin plagiarism software. Turnitin is used to identify copying and secondly, and more importantly here, to facilitate individual feedback on essay structure, writing style and referencing – a format successfully adopted in previous research (Ellery, 2008; Miller, 2009).

Process

Essay

When students had submitted their work in week 14, assignments were allocated to 50 tutors in the School. Each tutor was provided with detailed marking criteria, a model answer, guidance on feedback (including constructive criticisms on scripts)

1　For essay title and marking criteria, please see Appendix 1 and 2.

and guidance on using Turnitin (including how to use it for individual feedback and for advising the students).

When the assignments were marked, there was an extensive moderation process to ensure parity between members of staff so that students were marked fairly and accurately according to the criteria and feedback was provided consistently on their scripts.

Moderation involved all the tutors' marks (including means) being collated onto Microsoft Excel. Ten members of staff then volunteered to scrutinise samples of every tutor's marking to ensure marks were fair, consistent with other staff members marks and consistent with the marking criteria. All first-class marks and fails were considered, as were a percentage of 2:1, 2:2 and third class scripts. In total, 180 scripts (41%) were moderated. The outcome of the moderation process involved some changes to marks when these were considered to be too low or when critical comments on which marks were based were not relevant to the marking criteria.

Then the assignments were handed back to students, who were provided with feedback on their scripts, general feedback on a PowerPoint presentation (see Figure 1) and asked to speak to the tutor who had marked their work for more individual feedback (essay structure, writing style and referencing). Any students who failed this part of the assessment were required to use this feedback and resubmit within two weeks.

Figure 1 Example of general feedback given to students

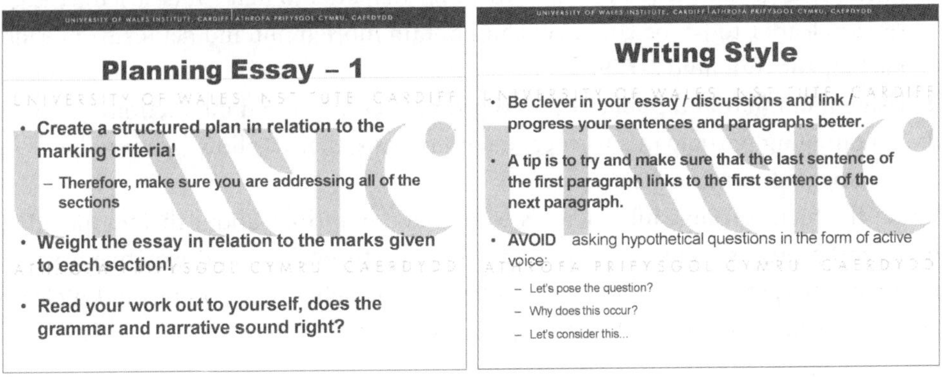

Planning Essay – 1

- Create a structured plan in relation to the marking criteria!
  - Therefore, make sure you are addressing all of the sections
- Weight the essay in relation to the marks given to each section!
- Read your work out to yourself, does the grammar and narrative sound right?

Writing Style

- Be clever in your essay / discussions and link / progress your sentences and paragraphs better.
- A tip is to try and make sure that the last sentence of the first paragraph links to the first sentence of the next paragraph.
- AVOID   asking hypothetical questions in the form of active voice:
  - Let's pose the question?
  - Why does this occur?
  - Let's consider this...

End of year exam

Tutors from each discipline who delivered this module over the two-week delivery blocks provided the researchers with the questions they had used. For example – about generating research questions, the different types of methods used to collect and analyse data and the strengths and issues of these methods as well as ethical considerations. Some of these were included in a formative assessment between week 22 and the end of module to give students experience in that type of assessment and to facilitate revision, whereas others were included in the multiple-choice exam that the students completed at the end of the academic year. Two examples of these questions include:

Q1   When a research question is identified, the methods should:
   a   lead the research question
   b   amend the research question
   c   be led by the research question
   d   be before the research question is identified.

Q2 Critiquing a journal article should primarily include an:
   a   evaluation of research justification, methods adopted, analysis used, and discussion
   b   evaluation of research justification, methods adopted, abstract, and analysis used
   c   evaluation of research justification, analysis used, and discussion
   d   evaluation of methods adopted, analysis used, and discussion.

Focus groups

To evaluate the module and the assessment and feedback strategy, six focus groups were conducted with Level 4 students at the end of the academic year. The focus groups followed the Barbour's (2007) guidelines and involved:

❑ Each participant being sent information on the topics that were to be covered before the focus group.

❑ Each focus group being limited to three participants to make it easier for the session leader to probe comments and obtain more input and details from each participant (Edmunds, 1999).

❑ Using a familiar and public room to promote comfort and interaction.

❑ Encouraging participants to engage with one another to allow issues to be investigated in more depth.

Within the focus groups, interviewees were asked questions about themes including the research process, the assessment structure (both positive and negative aspects), the learning experience (including how effective the delivery was in facilitating learning) and the key research skills developed at Level 4.

Evaluation

Multiple-choice exam and essay

Ninety-three percent of the students passed the multiple-choice assessment, averaging at 60.12% ($SD = 16.82$). At a first attempt, 82% of the students passed the essay assessment, averaging at 51.15% ($SD = 13.62$). Out of the 79 students that failed, 55 resubmitted within the two-week period and passed at the second attempt. Interestingly, as a deterrent for plagiarism, Turnitin results showed that only 10% of the cohort had values of over 30%, with the maximum value being 56% replication. Instead of reprimanding individuals who showed replication without paraphrasing or appropriate referencing, tutors were encouraged to guide the students through their mistakes, and were required to reinforce that any future unfair practice would be dealt with more severely.

Focus-group feedback

Focus groups were conducted at the end of the 2008–09 academic year and lasted over an hour each. After transcription, many themes were identified. Some of the themes that were consistently identified were:

- ❑ delivery
- ❑ relevance of essay assessment
- ❑ feedback from staff members
- ❑ availability of staff members to provide feedback
- ❑ the end of year exam.

In relation to delivery, students highlighted how going through the research process in each discipline was too repetitive. Specifically, some students were dissatisfied by the repetition of the research process on eight occasions via the different disciplines, as the following quote suggests:

> I think it got a bit dreary at times, because we had gone through something once and then we would do it again but with another discipline… it did hit home the point, but it was quite repetitive.

However, many students mentioned that focusing on the research process did benefit their understanding of 'research' and that the essay was relevant to the work that they met in the lectures:

> We [the students] were allowed to identify our own questions and work on them within all the disciplines – which was good. The essay required us to pretty much explain what we did during one of these two-week blocks, which helped my understanding of what was needed to be done.

Students had issues with feedback from staff members including illegible hand writing, lack of constructive comments and too many negative comments. Students also identified that some tutors were difficult to meet for further individual feedback, while some students mentioned that the model answer should have been made available earlier in the academic year. The following quote illuminates the impact that negative comments can have on the student experience:

> A lot of the feedback was bad, telling me what I did wrong. It made me think 'Why bother?' as I don't know what I'm supposed to take from these comments to learn. It would have been nice to know how I could do things better, especially how to write essays and reference properly.

On a positive side, many students highlighted that receiving individual feedback from staff members, which included seeing their Turnitin report, promoted understanding regarding adhering to marking criteria and writing more academically. In addition, for those students who failed, being provided with a model answer allowed them to more clearly visualise the marking criteria. The benefits of using model answers to promote learning has been demonstrated previously (Huxman, 2007), and is emphasised by this student's comment:

> I had never done this type of essay before so struggled with the first submission. [*The model answer*] helped my resubmission as I could finally see how to structure my essay.

Students thought that the end of year exam was not as challenging as the essay and that the positioning of the exam at the end of the year did not fully assess the progression that students go through after each discipline block. This is emphasised in the following quote:

> I thought it was pointless as I had forgotten a lot of what we did before Christmas. If we had shorter [*exams*] during the year then I think this would have helped me remember more about what we did with each discipline.

Discussion

Judging by the number of students who passed the essay and exam at the first attempt we can infer that, in general, students engaged with the new module design and assessment structure. Findings from the focus groups reinforce the importance of an assessment structure that is consistent with the content and delivery of a module, and that individual feedback is essential even when class sizes are large. Despite these encouraging findings, many lessons have been learned that will influence changes for the 2009–10 academic year.

Lessons learned

Based on feedback from students, the following changes will be made to the Level 4 *Research Methods* module for the 2009–10 academic year:

❑ To minimise repetition, the structure of delivery will be changed to two eight-week blocks, where students will be guided through the research process (a qualitative and a quantitative process) allowing the students to choose through which disciplines they will follow .

❑ The content and student tasks within each lecture will be consistent with the essay structure.

❑ Two tutors will deliver each lecture to promote discussion.

❑ The essay assessment will remain, but two summative Blackboard assessments will replace the end of year exam. These assessments will be at the end of each research block.

❑ Tutors will be supplied with training in Turnitin and providing appropriate feedback.

❑ Essays will be marked electronically, so that feedback can be more easily read by the students.

❑ We have also created a 'staff list' which provides students with the contact details of the tutors who marked their work.

Guidance

After completing the first year of this evolving redevelopment, the following guidance is offered to colleagues in other institutions – especially those who work with large cohorts and have a large teaching team:

❑ It is possible to create small-group environments within lecture theatres; however, it would seem that a team teaching strategy in lectures may better facilitate student learning in this environment.

❑ Students prefer continuous assessment and it enhances the student learning experience. With large numbers of students assessment is more manageable electronically; in addition, the use of electronic feedback tackles complaints about illegible feedback.

❑ Managing large numbers of tutors is a difficult process, especially with regards to the quality and consistency of feedback – which includes marking to the criteria and being available to provide feedback directly to students. Providing detailed guidance to staff minimises these issues but there is still a need to provide staff development on such issues.

❑ Qualitative methods are a valuable tool to attain feedback from students regarding module design, delivery, and assessment.

References

Barbour, R. (2007) *Doing focus groups*. Sage: London

Edmunds, H. (1999) *The focus group research handbook*. Chicago, IL: NTC Business Books

Ellery, K. (2008) An investigation into electronic-source plagiarism in a first year essay assignment. *Assessment & Evaluation in Higher Education* 33 607–17

Huxman, M. (2007) Fast and effective feedback: Are model answers the answer? *Assessment & Evaluation in Higher Education* 32 601–11

Miller, T. (2009) Formative computer-based assessment in higher education: the effectiveness of feedback in supporting student learning. *Assessment & Evaluation in Higher Education* 34 181–92

DR RICH NEIL is Discipline Director of Research Methods and Senior Lecturer in Sport Psychology at the Cardiff School of Sport, UWIC. His research interests include competition stress, competitive anxiety, self-confidence, hardiness and the management of diabetes.

DR KYLIE WILSON is the Programme Director for BSc (Hons) *Sport and Physical Education* and Lecturer in Exercise Psychology at the University of Wales Institute, Cardiff. Her research interests include achievement goal orientations, motivational climate, and leadership and communication within teams.

DR RICHARD TONG is the director of learning & teaching and deputy dean in the Cardiff School of Sport at UWIC. He is also the sport liaison officer for the H E Academy Subject Centre for Hospitality, Leisure, Sport and Tourism. He is the chair of the Education & Professional Development Division for the British Association of Sport & Exercise Science and the moderator champion for learning & teaching for the University of Wales. His research interests and publications are in sports physiology, pedagogy and assessment

Appendices

Appendix 1:   Essay Title / Student Guidelines

Choose a relevant issue related to your programme of study and attempt to explain how research might help us to understand the issue better.

Structure your essay in the following order:

1   Identify a relevant issue and state why this issue is important for coaches, sport scientists, sports development officers, physical education specialists OR society in general.

Key words: Knowledge, evidence, informed, objective, scientific, substantiated, truth, interpretation, understanding.

2   Define research and explain what makes research different to opinion or speculation.

Key words: Systematic, rigorous, fair, honest, reliable, valid, true, evidenced.

3   Identify four specific research questions that, once answered, could contribute to our understanding of the problem (also briefly identify how they would improve our understanding of the problem).

Key points: Specific, measurable, achievable, realistic. They must be questions not statements.

4   Choose one of these questions and identify which academic discipline/disciplines will provide the theoretical underpinning to the research.

Disciplines might include: history, psychology, physiology, notational analysis, sociology, philosophy, management, biomechanics, and pedagogy.

Theoretical underpinning might include: motivation, gender, oxygen uptake, or another specific discipline based framework for understanding sport.

5   Explain how you would operationalise your research question in order to collect specific kind of data (be explicit with the type of data).

Design

Is the research descriptive, predictive, explanatory, exploratory?

Sample

What sample would you use?

Instrumentation

What questions, tests, or archives would you use?

Data Analysis

For analysis, are you looking at differences, relationships, correlations, indicative, generalisations?

Is the data quantitative or qualitative and why?

6   Identify and discuss one problem with validity, one with reliability and one

with ethics that might be encountered in the research process.

Validity

Are you measuring what you say you are?

Key words: true, believable, significant, credible, objective, thorough, trustworthy, honest and fair.

Reliability

Are you measuring it accurately and reliably?

Key words: Replicable, Repeated observations or re-test reliability, interobserver reliability.

Ethics

Are you measuring it in a way that ensures the psychological, social, physical well-being of the object of research and the researcher themselves?

Key words: Informed consent, privacy, safety, honesty, the value of the study.

When writing the essay, ensure that:

❏ Five peer reviewed journal articles are included to help to inform the design of your question / project. Include the abstracts for each paper an appendix.

❏ You write in an academic essay style and reference correctly.

Word Length:	1200
Submission Date:	Week 14
Marked by:	Week 18
Returned to Students by:	Week 19
Resubmission (2nd sit) by:	Week 21
Returned to Students by:	Week 22

Appendix 2:   Essay Marking Criteria for Staff

	Criteria	**Purpose**
1	¶ A relevant problem / issue in sport / health / or dance is identified ¶ A clear statement is also provided about why this issue is important for coaches, sport scientists, sports development officers, physical education specialists, dance community, OR society in general. Key words to look for: *Knowledge, understanding, applied practice.*	¶ To get students to think about problems that are worthy of researching in sport / health / dance. ¶ To get students to justify why it is important to look at problems from a knowledge development and applied perspective.
2	¶ The term Research has been defined. ¶ A reference should be provided to support this definition. ¶ The term Research is explained in relation to what makes research different to opinion or speculation. Key words to look for: *Process, Systematic, rigorous, reliable, valid, evidenced.*	¶ To promote understanding of research as a systematic process ¶ To get students to include references to support key definitions
3	¶ FOUR specific research questions (not statements) are identified that, once answered, could contribute to our understanding of the problem. ¶ These questions should be more specific than the research problem identified in Part 1 of the essay and can be in any discipline. Key words to look for: *Specific, measurable, achievable, realistic.*	¶ To get students to think about more specific, measurable questions from general issues. ¶ To get students to realise that a general problem can be addressed by many questions and/or disciplines.
4	¶ One of these questions is then chosen and related to a specific academic discipline/ disciplines that will provide the theoretical underpinning to the research ¶ A peer reviewed reference(s) should be provided that illuminates the research question. Disciplines include: History, psychology, physiology, notational analysis, sociology, philosophy, management, development, biomechanics, conditioning, coaching. Theoretical underpinning might include: motivation, gender, oxygen uptake, or another discipline based framework/theory for understanding sport.	¶ To get students to identify disciplines that may help to inform their specific question. ¶ To get students to identify a theory within the chosen discipline that may help to inform the specific question. ¶ To get students to include peer reviewed research articles to inform specific question.

Criteria	Purpose	
¶ Students should explain how they would operationlise their research question in order to collect specific kind of data	¶ To get students to think about how they would address the question they have chosen.	15
¶ Specifically, a general overview of what type of research it would be and how they may go about collecting data	¶ To get students to identify previous research that has used similar approaches (to justify their own approach)	
¶ A peer reviewed reference(s) should be provided to inform the given approach		
¶ Design: The student should identify and explain whether the research is descriptive, predictive, explanatory, exploratory		
¶ Sample: The Student should identify the sample and why they have chosen them?		
¶ Instrumentation: The Student should identify, generally, how the data will be collected. That is, through questionnaires, interviews, tests, archives etc.		
¶ Data Analysis: The students should identify whether they are looking at differences, relationships, correlations, indicative, explanations, in depth insight, etc.		
¶ Students must identify and describe one problem with validity, one with reliability, and one ethical issue that might be encountered in the research process.	¶ To get students to think about issues with methods they choose to adopt.	15
¶ Validity – are you measuring what you say you are?	¶ Specifically, to get students to identify factors that could affect validity and reliability, along with one ethical issue.	

Key words to look for: *true, believable, significant, credible, objective, thorough, trustworthy, honest and fair.*

¶ Reliability – are you measuring it accurately and reliably?

Key words to look for: *Replicable, Repeated observations, re- test and inter-observer reliability.*

¶ Ethics – are you measuring it in a way that ensures the psychological, social, physical well- being of the object of research and the researcher themselves?

Key words to look for: *Informed consent, risk of harm, rights to service, voluntary.*

¶ Students must write in an academic essay style and reference correctly (refer to CSS Student Handbook).	¶ To get students to write in a more academic prose.	15
	¶ To get students to look at Student Handbooks and writing material (i.e., guides) that are available in the library.	

These are the Marking Criteria for the Level 4 Research Methods Essay. Please provide marks based on each aspect of the criteria and provide comments (both critical and constructive) on the scripts.

12

Exploring the 'myths' of enhanced learning through group-work assessment

Helen Pokorny *University of Westminster* and
David Griffiths *London Metropolitan University*

This chapter explores the complexities of the group-work assessment process. Recently the incidence of group-work assessment has risen, to offer a way to reduce the assessment load for staff and deliver the benefits of collaborative working and team-building skills. In an attempt to parallel the student experience the authors explored the conditions that affect the use of group work as a tool to enhance learning through assessment.

Introduction

The chapter draws on the reflections of a group of staff attempting to parallel the experience of students participating in group work as an assessment tool, and compares the data generated from a staff and student survey on group work with the staff reflections on their own group work process. Through our case study we explore some of the 'myths' about group-work assessment as set out in a paper by Livingstone and Lynch (2000: 327). These are:

1　'Clever' students do not get sufficient credit for their work.
2　Unequal contributions from team members unfairly affect grades.
3　Lazy students can 'hide' from staff members.
4　Group work slows down the learning process due to unproductive time such as meetings.
5　Group work impacts on other work due to the extra demands on student time.
6　Group composition unfairly affects one group over another, for example, skills make-up, personality clashes.

We challenge the view that these are 'myths' by highlighting some of the issues inherent in our experience and raising questions about the prevalence of group work as a means of assessment. Rather they are the reality for many students.

Objectives

In order to achieve a greater understanding of the issues facing students when they attempt an assessed piece of group work we set ourselves the task of producing a joint conference paper with a deadline of eight weeks as a means of simulating a student 'assessed' group work task. We monitored our group processes as we worked on this and on a joint research project investigating staff and student responses to group work through an on-line questionnaire survey.

From the outset, and in achieving the tasks we set ourselves, we examined our own engagement with the group process. The findings from the data provided some interesting parallels and insights into the pressures and experiences of group work, which were compared to data from the staff and student responses. We considered the effects of using profiling tools on the dynamics of our group; the impact of external interventions on the group; the contributions made by different members of the group; and how assessment impacts on group processes and dynamics. Our analysis led us to question whether the pressures of the assessment process might not potentially undermine the benefits of group work activity and collaborative learning, and encouraged us to highlight the lessons learned from our experiences.

Rationale

Livingstone and Lynch (2000) compared two different forms of group-work assessment, one intended to simulate the workplace directly and a second, more conventional written assessment and in doing so questioned what they called the 'myths' of group work, numbered in our introduction. We decided to examine these myths in the light of our own experiences and the responses given to us by the students.

Context

Our research was undertaken in the business school of an inner-city post-1992 university which has a highly culturally diverse student population. The school has around 9,500 students on undergraduate and postgraduate programmes. At least 2,000 of these are international students and additionally there are some 1,900 European students. The remainder of the students are largely local and reflect the cosmopolitan population of London. Group-work assessment is a feature of postgraduate and undergraduate courses with some lecturers making more extensive use of the approach than others. Of the final year students we surveyed, 46% had been asked to provide a single piece of assessed written work as a group task. It was this process that we considered alongside our own experience of producing a joint conference paper.

Description

Our practice-oriented case study seeks to throw light on some of the mechanics and dynamics which can impact on the production of assessed group work. It draws on ethnographic perspectives, which rely on the involvement of the researchers in the project and their insider observations. Alvesson's (2003) discussion of the use of self-ethnography for higher education research provides justification for the importance of such approaches. The researchers' closeness to the data is therefore imperative in providing the reality of the group work experience.

Staff case study data

We generated the data necessary to present an evaluative analysis of our staff group processes by using information from a variety of sources as follows:

❑ notes and transcripts of group meetings
❑ group members' public and private blogs
❑ personal profiling instruments:
   Myers-Briggs type inventory (MBTI), FIRO-B inventory (Schutz, 1958), Belbin team role inventory (Belbin, 2003)
❑ personal reflective narratives.

Survey data

Additionally, we collected on-line survey data from 45 tutors across the business school and from 63 final-year business school students on different single-honours programmes of study. We asked about their experiences and perceptions of group-work assessment. This survey data has been reported as triangulation for the findings from our staff-group work experiences.

Discussion

The following discussion is developed in relation to our own reflections and in the context of comparisons with the reported student experiences and the 'myths' identi-fied by Livingstone and Lynch (2000).

Group formation

Different options are offered in the educational literature for allocating students to groups. These are broadly, an ad hoc allocation by tutor, allocation by tutor accord-ing to some criterion or self-selecting. Our staff group was self-selecting and was comprised of four people brought together by one member who knew, and had worked with, the other three. When comparing this with the student experience we found that 83% of the student respondents indicated that their assessment groups were also self-selecting. However despite choosing to work with a particular group of students, the process was still problematic in many cases, and 33% said their group 'worked badly together'. When asked if they would like to work in the same group again 37% said 'not at all' and only 19% said that they would 'very much like to do so.'

Unlike student assessment, our staff group was not only self-selecting but also voluntary so that, although we committed to working together, any one member could have withdrawn from the group without sanction, leaving the others to com-plete the process. As such the power dynamics and levels of autonomy in our group were fundamentally different from those of students for whom success in assessed group work is reflected in grades. At the outset, exactly how each member of our staff group would contribute was not clear. Each member had specific, defined, work roles but there was still a need to negotiate how individual members could best contribute to the project, which required getting to know each other.

It took two meetings for the staff group to start to gel. After the first meeting, members reported feeling variously unsure of what they could offer personally, feeling pressured and anxious, as well as optimistic, thinking that 'we might achieve something' and 'maybe thinking this was not such a good idea after all'. The 'untold stories' of group work came from an analysis of the members' personal narratives of the process. We have reflected on these using Tuckman's (1965) definition of group stages:

Forming
The group comes together and gets to initially know one other and form as a group.

Storming
A chaotic vying for leadership and trialling of group processes.

Norming
Eventually agreement is reached on how the group operates.

Performing
The group becomes effective in meeting its objectives.

We observed from the narratives how difficult the initial 'forming' stage of the process was:

> I was really surprised by how trepidatious I was at that first meeting, I was really scared, that's the truth... you were a complete unknown quantity. I was quite worried about meeting you, and I'd already met you, and the funny thing X, was that you were the one who scared me the most because you seemed so dynamic and switched on, seriously... I felt vulnerable and I don't mean anything against anybody in this group, it's just that I didn't know (X) very well and I didn't know Y very well. I knew who you were, and obviously I knew Z but not through working together. So I think I felt quite vulnerable.

After the second meeting, we saw that a sense of 'forming' began to take place. Mutual trust was developing. However, it was easy to see how students might be silenced by feelings similar to those expressed above and why, despite possible drawbacks, they might choose to work with the same group over time.

A key lesson for us was recognising the importance of the social aspect of our working together. A significant proportion of meeting time was devoted to maintaining and developing relationships, and this was something that required time over and above that of working on the task. It was, however, felt that the social aspect was central to the group work and not a by-product. One member commented specifically

> I now think of you as three great friends really, and that's important for me to work in this kind of atmosphere, I can't work if I'm not friendly with the people I

work with.

Livingstone and Lynch (2000) suggest that it may be a myth that 'Group composition unfairly affects one group over another, for example, skills make-up, personality clashes'. They suggest that allocating students to specific roles can help to avoid this myth, replacing Tuckman's (1965) group formation stages of forming, storming and norming and taking students straight to the performing stage. Whilst allocating roles may help to clarify actions more quickly from a task perspective, in terms of group process, even if roles are allocated, the group still requires time to 'form' and that the issues of skills make-up and personality clashes can dominate the process and hence the outcome.

Time

Lack of time was a huge issue for our staff group. Livingstone and Lynch (2000: 327) suggest that it may be myth that, 'Group work slows down the learning process due to unproductive time such as meetings.' Even though we worked in the same institution, meetings were extremely difficult to arrange.

Time is a hugely limiting factor particularly in institutions with a diverse cohort where students have complex and stressful lives and may be combining significant employment and caring responsibilities with full-time study. In our survey 59% of students reported that 'not everyone attended the group meetings regularly' and 80% of those respondents reported that this had been 'a problem for the group.' It seems an important lesson to ensure that, where group work is assessed time is allocated for meeting in-class. Only 5% of our student respondents had undertaken 'most of their meetings during class time.'

Fifty-six per cent of students identified face-to-face meetings as their preferred means of communication. Similarly our staff group elected to postpone meetings several times when one member could not attend, which resulted in increasing gaps in face-to-face discussions and slippage of deadlines. Email was used to try to supplement communication but this was not always effective. The volume and nature of the email communications meant that some went unacknowledged or could only be dealt with in a cursory manner. It became clear how it might be that 'Group work impacts on other work due to the extra demands on student time' (Livingstone and Lynch, 2000: 327) without specific times to meet up.

Profiling and reflection

Key issues were observed in relation to reflection, some of which were linked to profiling. In both the workplace and for student group work assessment one of the common profiling tools used to support the group inter-relations process is Belbin's (2003) team roles inventory. Belbin proposes that if all team roles are filled, the group will work harmoniously and effectively. The staff group profiling exercises started in the second meeting. We began with Belbin and also used the Schutz (1958)

FIRO-B questionnaire which proposes three basic needs/dimensions of interpersonal relations:

❑ Inclusion – the need for belongingness and interaction
❑ Control – the need for influence
❑ Affection – the need for intimacy and friendship.

We then completed the Myers-Briggs type indicator (MBTI) – an indicator of one's 'style', for example, of seeking information ('big picture' versus 'detail') and making judgements ('logic' versus 'values/feelings').

The profiles were completed in the group members' own time and then shared in a meeting guided by the group member who had expertise in interpreting such profiles. Interestingly, the time devoted to sharing these profiles was short and discussions limited to a few very brief observations. 'We did have a quick look but we didn't look at it in a sort of bonding affirming way, we just really sneaked a look.' The level of discomfort reported in this activity was high:

> I felt quite vulnerable when I came to the group and that was enhanced when we
> did the profiles. I think that was the peak of my discomfort.

It was observed in subsequent discussions that there was a tendency to use humour and exaggeration when discussing the profiles, 'I came out as a manic extrovert who's bossy!' (an observation made about the MBTI). Despite one group member being a profiling expert, at no stage were these exercises used in a conscious and pro-active manner to aid the group's development. We found that our experience was similar to 83% of the student respondents, in that the profiling took place at the outset of the process but was not referred to subsequently.

One of the staff group members noted that there was no one in the Belbin role who would help to shape the 'mental map' of the group and suggested that this might have explained why the group were all feeling unsure of their purpose and direction. Another member commented: 'I'm not sure that we've got on top of that feeling despite ploughing on with activities.' This was an issue for both the research project and the conference paper. When the staff group reflected on this, it was clear that the research project was shaped over time through discussion and negotiation, as there was a high degree of autonomy and flexibility. Outcomes evolved rather than being shaped by the intervention of any one individual. In contrast, the production of the conference paper was constrained by the title, abstract and deadline.

Group members discussed the notion of profiles being used to shape the 'ideal' group 'but the problem is you are always short of completer-finishers or whatever'. This might be perceived as self-limiting from the outset. Profiling can also be seen as a normalising process with inventories such as Belbin's providing a self-regulating tool predicated on the basis that a 'good' team provides 'a place for everyone and everyone in their place'. Ritter (2007: 569) has noted how such profiles have the 'reductionist effect of promoting commonality'. This espoused commonality may contrast with the real experience of many groups and encourage the view that such lived experience is deviant or 'wrong' and should be hidden.

One outcome of profiling may be that in order to conform to the 'ideal', problems with group process may be glossed over and become invisible to the assessor, perhaps even more so if reflections on the group process are themselves assessed by the tutor, which was the case for 57% of our tutor respondents. Dyke (2006: 116) highlights that

> reflection in learning needs to be open and concerned with weakness as well as strengths, while assessment by its very nature is concerned with the presentation of strengths.

The process of reflection on interpersonal relationships is daunting even for those who know each other. It is something that, at work, is generally undertaken individually and in private. Public reflection, which is often a requirement of assessment, is a difficult and uncomfortable process.

The fact that the profiling typologies were not really referred to or used again resonates with the experience of many of our student respondents, with 83% of students indicating that they had completed a profile which their tutor had not referred to in class. Furthermore we would suggest that without a long-term developmental context and expertise, profiling can risk damaging the student's self esteem. Belbin's model is contextual and people adopt different roles around the context, nature and make up of the team (Belbin Associates, 2009), hence his model might be more helpful as a reflective tool rather than as a tool used at the start of group work without further reference.

Participation and reflection

One of the most telling insights gained from this process related to issues around equality of participation. Livingstone and Lynch suggest that it may be a myth that:

> Clever students do not get sufficient credit for their work.
>
> Unequal contributions from team members unfairly affect grades.
>
> Lazy students can 'hide' from staff members (2000: 327).

We were particularly interested in exploring these notions of 'unfairness', 'unequal contributions' and 'freeloaders', which Gunn (cited in Bloxham and Boyd 2007: 59) defines as 'generally represented by ...[some group member(s)] seeming unengaged whilst others seem to be doing all the work.'

In our student survey 58% of students did not feel that everyone in the group had contributed equally and 37% replied 'not at all' when asked if they would want to work with the same group again. Their answers to the follow-up question, 'why not?' related to issues of unequal contributions, for example,

> I felt that some have not put in as much effort resulting in us receiving a lower grade... Some students take advantage and input very little or very last minute. This is not fair... You also feel bad informing the tutor especially when the other

group member may deny all or use excuses as they did with me.

Although, for the staff group, differential contributions were an integral feature of both undertaking the research project and writing the conference paper, the nature of the conference paper exercise – which can be seen as a proxy for assessment – served to exclude and marginalise participation and introduced a different set of dynamics, with unequal power relations.

For example, we have already noted that time was a huge issue for us both individually and collectively. There were many unexpected pressures, professional and personal, that inhibited individual contributions. Tellingly one member noted; 'I would say that would be one of the key things for me is that what I've discovered is that you can feel terribly guilty and still not do anything.' The group worked on the research project to individual strengths and availability, members co-operated, went away and undertook actions (or not), came back and discussed them. Collaboration was an important part of the process, but not central to actually getting the work done. Different perspectives were prized and individuals focused on making their own contributions.

In contrast, for the paper, it was necessary to produce a single point of view and the differential inputs were stark. In fact it became impossible to participate equally. This meant that some points of view were silenced as others dominated, although this silencing could perhaps have been interpreted differently – as 'freeloading'. With the deadline for the conference paper looming there was pressure to work together on the task. It was agreed that the group would meet, commandeer a computer and try to plan the paper together initially, then email the text round. Arranging this meeting was very difficult with all members under major time pressures.

At the beginning of the meeting, one member unexpectedly offered some advice from a colleague outside the group on how the group should proceed and what the anticipated outcomes should be. The impact was evidenced from the pauses in the transcript and resulted in a loss of impetus. One member left saying: 'I really don't think this meeting was helpful.' Comments from others included, 'what's going on? I thought we were meeting to write the paper? The discussion felt irrelevant...loss of trust and confidentiality.' The meeting was unproductive although some notes were made.

Interestingly, given the importance often attached to acknowledging and working through Tuckman's (1965) 'conflict' stage, one member saw the meeting quite differently:

> We talk about a crisis meeting. I went away from that meeting not realising that any of that had gone on until X told me afterwards...I hadn't realised the boiling, seething bit! Why didn't I notice it? That worried me afterwards'.

The outcome was that two of the group took on the writing with other members commenting to a greater or (much) lesser extent, and some members feeling unable to participate in the process.

> I think I dominated the writing process...I need time to read and think and write...
> I find I can't easily fit into a round-robin process of writing.

This is probably the reality of most assessed group writing. It became clear that it is probably impossible to maintain the dialogue needed to think and write jointly in groups of more than two. It may be argued that the synthesising of ideas and perspectives is not a requirement of a particular group work assessment, in which case we would suggest that questions need to be asked about what is learned by individual students in relation to the learning outcomes. Additionally, from our staff-group experience, we learned that the impact of an external or tutor intervention in group work, particularly at times of stress, may not prove helpful. In our particular case, where there had been no earlier interventions, the late intervention almost derailed our group entirely. We learned that the ongoing active monitoring of the group process by the tutor is important in order that the tutor can make helpful, timely interventions.

Our staff experience also led us to seriously question the validity of written group work assessment as a means of testing knowledge and understanding. We found that 96% of our tutor respondents assessed the group product and 57% assessed the group process. Our staff experience would suggest that it is very likely that what is graded as a group product reflects the learning of some group member(s) more accurately than others. Many of the tutor respondents acknowledged that it is very difficult to apportion differential marks across a group although 34% of them did so on occasions using a variety of self and peer assessment processes. One tutor commented:

> Nominally there was an internal group assessment – group members assessing each other. It hasn't so far yielded any insights, despite a couple of quite dysfunctional groups.

We have already suggested above that non-contributing students may be afraid of being penalised, and reluctant to share their experiences publicly; one tutor responded:

> I feel very strongly that the problem of freeloading is given too great a priority compared to that of the marginalisation of group members.

Conclusions

As a result of the analysis of our group experiences our conclusions are that student group work as an assessment activity imposes an additional layer of complexity and constraint that can impede the benefits of group-based learning. The assessment outcome is dependant on many variables outside the individual student's control: the emotional intelligence of all parties, time, social and cultural contexts. The interdependence and limited control and management of these issues in assessment may well result in unequal contributions and accusations of 'freeloading'. Students may or may not be 'lazy'. 'I didn't do very much unless I was ordered to and I did rely on X to nag me to do things.' Equally a lack of contribution may well be because of exclusion from the group through time pressures and/or the social and cultural dynamics of the group situation.

Our findings provide some insights into the pressures and power dynamics that students may experience when asked to jointly produce piece of written assessment. They are particularly important in the context of student diversity and widening participation where students may have very different cultural and social backgrounds adding further to the challenge of the process.

Our analysis suggests to us that what may be seen as the myths of group work (Livingstone and Lynch, 2000) are, on the contrary, the reality for many groups. In promoting the process without clear regard to these issues we may be promoting an assessment process that militates against real team-building and collaborative learning. Furthermore it may have an irretrievable impact upon an individual student's module grade. For these reasons we would argue that the use of written group work assessment should be considered carefully in the context of the course and module learning outcomes and the time available and that it should be actively planned, monitored and managed by the tutor in order to pre-empt as far as possible some of the issues outlined in this chapter.

References

Alvesson, M. (2003) 'Methodology for close up studies – struggling with closeness and closure.' *Higher Education* **46** pp 167–93

Belbin Associates (2009) *Method, Reliability & Validity, Statistics & Research: A Comprehensive Review of Belbin Team Roles*. Accessible at http://www.belbin.com/content/page/4279/BELBIN-MRVSR-AComprehensiveReview-2009.pdf

Belbin, R. M. (2003) *Management Teams – Why They Succeed or Fail* (2nd edition). Oxford: Butterworth-Heinemann

Bloxham, S. and Boyd, P. (2007) *Developing Effective Assessment in Higher Education: A Practical Guide*. Open University Press

Dyke, M. (2006) The role of the 'other' in reflection, knowledge formation and action in late modernity. *International Journal of Lifelong Education* **25** (2) March-April 105–23

Livingstone, D. & Lynch, K. (2000) Group Project Work and Student-centred Active Learning: two different experiences. *Studies in Higher Education* **25** (3) pp. 325–45

MBTI. MBTI, Myers-Briggs and Myers-Briggs Type Indicator are trademarks or registered trademarks of the Myers-Briggs Type Indicator Trust in the United States accessible at http://www.myersbriggsreports.com/

Ritter, L. (2007) Unfulfilled promises: how inventories, instruments and institutions subvert discourses of diversity and promote commonality. *Teaching in Higher Education* **12** (5-6) pp 569–79

Schutz, W. (1958) *FIRO: A Three-Dimensional Theory of Interpersonal Behaviour*. New York: Holt, Rinehart & Winston,.

Tuckman, B. W. (1965) Developmental sequence in small groups. *Psychological Bulletin* **63** (6) pp 384–99

HELEN POKORNY is a principal lecturer, learning and teaching in the Westminster Exchange at the University of Westminster. Her interests are in examining the social context within which assessment takes place. She has written on the student experience of feedback, group work assessment, the assessment of prior experiential learning (APEL) and curriculum development in relation to student diversity.

DAVID GRIFFITHS works in the Centre for Academic and Professional Development at London Metropolitan University, teaching on in-house professional, learning and teaching courses. Before joining the university eleven years ago he worked for many years as an HR staff development manager in the public and charity sectors and has extensive experience of facilitating Action Learning sets and other group-based activities.

Acknowledgement – We would like to acknowledge the important contribution made to our work by our friends and colleagues Pamela Pickford and Jan Bamford for their wisdom, insight and humour.

13

Using oral debriefing to assess student learning in a business simulation game

Jonathan Lean and Jonathan Moizer
University of Plymouth Business School

This chapter examines the use of oral debriefing with role-play as a means for assessment on a strategic management module for postgraduate, post experience, part-time students. The oral debriefing focuses on students' experiences of running their own companies within a business simulation game.

Introduction

The University of Plymouth Business School (PBS) has a history of using simulation games (SGs) to teach across a number of business management subjects including corporate strategy, financial management, shipping and logistics, and hospitality management. Student learning from gaming is assessed using a mixture of game performance and post-gaming written or oral debriefing.

We had three objectives. Firstly, we sought to discuss how role-play assessment is designed and structured around the intended learning outcomes (ILOs) set for this module. The second objective was to evaluate the assessment approach, drawing on relevant literature on the importance of debriefing exercises for reflective learning when using SGs. Our third objective was to consider the challenges and benefits of assessing student learning using this approach.

Rationale

The benefits of employing business simulation games (SGs) to help develop decision-making skills are well established (see Moizer et al, 2006; Edelheim & Ueda, 2007). SGs can bring experiential learning into the classroom. Such learning is often deeper than that achieved when conventional approaches are adopted, with the opportunity for learning to occur at all levels in Bloom's taxonomy (Anderson & Lawton, 1988). As well as often being perceived as more fun by students, SGs provide a means of integrating subject matter into the mainstream of students' interests.

An SG can be viewed as a 'learning laboratory' where experimentation can be achieved and understandings of the nature of cause-and-effect developed. SGs can correspond with reality; but at the same time provide a safe environment for students to play out risks and live with the consequences. Students attain a level of ownership in which they move from passive to active learners. They are presented with the opportunity to put the theories they learn into action.

Business academics are served well by a market of off-the-shelf computer-based business games. In particular, there is a plentiful supply of strategic management or 'total enterprise games' that can be integrated into the teaching syllabus and be used to help students to achieve the ILOs of a strategic management module.

Interactive role-play can be part and parcel of a simulation gaming experience. Commonly with business SGs, participants and instructors act out the role of characters in the gaming situation (students as decision-makers and instructors as actors residing outside the company). The students often assume prescribed roles in the gaming situation, for example, managing director or director of finance. In role-play, students attempt to develop an understanding of circumstances and roles that are beyond their immediate experience (Sutcliffe, 2002). The students are given the opportunity to feel what is at stake. It is hoped that better understanding of roles and relationships and a greater awareness of their own activities emerges from a role-play experience.

Getting students to reflect post-play on the knowledge gained holistically from SGs, and on how the various strands of information fit together, can help promote deeper learning. Knotts and Keys (1997) argue that, most frequently, learning occurs when participants are forced to reflect on their experiences. This process of reflection can be facilitated through debriefing. Debriefing makes the link between the game itself and the achievement of learning outcomes (Garris et al, 2002). Debriefing provides the opportunity to review and analyse the events that occurred during the gaming cycle. It allows the knowledge gleaned from game-play to be consolidated, and for argumentation to be developed and assessed (Sutcliffe, 2002). Oral debriefing conducted in-role can be extremely valuable, as it allows the realism of the experience to be extended. Arguably, in this situation, the gaming participants are still thinking and acting as decision-makers and thus they are able to reflect more easily on the past, present and future direction of their company.

Within the process of a post-game oral role-play debriefing, summative assessment can be used to measure the extent to which student participants have learned about managing company strategy in a complex business environment. Provided that the assessment is aligned to the module ILOs, a debriefing activity can not only allow good reflection but can also measure the extent to which students have learnt from the gaming experience.

Context

The University of Plymouth Business School runs a number of postgraduate, post-experience programmes of study to serve the professional development needs of managers from across south-west England. One of these programmes is the Diploma in Management Studies (DMS), a Level 7 qualification. The ILOs for this programme are challenging and students need to demonstrate their achievement of these higher-order learning outcomes on each module.

Diploma in Management Studies students are taught strategic management as a capstone subject, dovetailing the various strands of business and management studies. The mode of delivery previously followed the traditional model of formal lectures with accompanying student-led case-study orientated seminars. The teaching material sought to introduce an understanding of the development of strategic visioning and mission, the setting of business objectives, the crafting of strategy, its implementation, and finally the principles of performance measurement, environmental monitoring and control. It was apparent that most students gained a good understanding of how many of the tools and frameworks could be used to analyse the business environment and the strengths and weaknesses of a given company.

However, difficulties in comprehension surfaced which centred upon students' critical evaluation and application of the possible strategic options relevant to a given case study. The academics were of the opinion that case studies might have been producing learning that centred on lower-order skills. This may have been because of the static composition of many written cases. The opportunity to explore the effects of a range of alternative decisions within a dynamic business environment was less achievable within such a framework. The desire was to avoid leading students towards a view that the practice of strategy is simply mechanistic, and that it can be delivered through applying a range of two-dimensional frameworks.

Instead, we sought to emphasise in the teaching the possible outcomes arising from alternative streams of strategic decisions. After discussion and reflection among the academic staff, simulation gaming was proposed as an option for supporting the teaching of strategy. This decision mirrored a general movement in the school over several years towards the practice of active learning. It was against this backdrop that we introduced the use of SGs to teach strategy in a more experiential way.

Mindful of the need to provide a real-world feel to teaching and learning, we sought to develop a mode of summative assessment in keeping with the gaming approach. Hence, rather than requiring the students to debrief on the game learning experience through writing a management report or delivering a presentation, we decided to use a mixed written and oral debriefing method, where the reflective learning would emanate from an 'across the table' structured discussion.

Description

A number of criteria were set for the selection and adoption of a computer-based strategy game (SG):

❑ fidelity to the real-world of strategic management
❑ technical robustness

❑ ability to engage students in team-based learning over a sustained period
❑ capacity to help deliver module ILOs
❑ potential for student assessment.

The Business Strategy Game

After a review of various commercially available games, the SG that best matched the criteria was *The Business Strategy Game* (BSG) by Thompson et al (2009). This was selected for integration into the teaching syllabus for the strategic management module.

The BSG is a web-based total enterprise simulation game that can be accessed 24/7 from any computer with an internet connection. The game is strategic in nature and is based upon a global business engaged in the manufacture and sale of athletic footwear. Student teams (or companies) compete against each other for a predetermined pattern of market demand. An instructor is responsible for overseeing the running of the game and sets up many of the externalities which will shape company decision-making (such as exchange rates, material prices and shipping costs).

The game requires the input of yearly business decisions, such as volumes of goods to manufacture, shipment volumes, pricing levels and advertising spend. These decisions are collectively processed on an on-line server program, and the game then rolls on to another year's play. Scores based on a number of performance metrics (for example, profit, market share, capitalisation, sales volume) are determined, resulting in the teams moving up or down a league table. The BSG can be run over a sustained series of decision periods (simulated years).

The process of using the business strategy game

There are a number of activities involved in introducing students to the BSG, getting them to play the game and helping them to reflect on their learning experience. Table 1 outlines the five stages involved in managing the BSG process.

Table 1 Pedagogic approach adopted

Key Stages in Using the SG	Outline of Activities
Stage One: Briefing	Initial lecture introducing the BSG and its links to the study module
Stage Two: Company formation	Teams of two or three students selected per company
Stage Three: Familiarisation	Reading of the supplementary BSG literature
Stage Four: Gaming	Playing out company decisions over the gaming period
Stage Five: Debriefing	Reflective meetings between the individual companies and the instructors where role-play oral assessment takes place

It is essential to a well-constructed briefing (Kriz, 2008; Edelheim and Ueda, 2007) to introduce the nature of the SGs, along with relevant learning objectives, any assessment criteria, gaming rules and the general mechanisms of play. The student briefing comprises an introduction to the ILOs associated with the game, how the gaming activity is assessed, the game background, its rules, and the meaning and interpretation of data outputs.

Students are asked to form teams and adopt the role of company directors. Next, students familiarise themselves with the game's parameters and rules through reading the accompanying players' guide. Participants are then free to explore the simulation game and develop strategies to beat their competitors. The teams input a range of quantitative decisions into a computer to cover finance and investment, human resources, production and operations, logistics and distribution, and sales and promotion activities for their companies.

Decision-making continues throughout the remaining playing period. Interim feedback on each team's progress is available after each 'yearly' gaming round. The interim reports generated on company performance provide an opportunity for the instructor to provide in-game debriefing. It is important that the instructor does not direct the teams in their decision-making, but through informal discussion the opportunity does exist to offer some feedback in order to help students understand the structure and dynamics of their simulated environment and consolidate their learning experience.

Post-game debriefing

The final, and arguably most critical, stage in the pedagogic process is the debriefing exercise. As the student teams are so busy running their simulated companies over the gaming period (which typically lasts for six to ten weeks), they do not get much chance to solidify their learning from the game until they reflect on the experience, post-play. Debriefing does require a structured facilitation process with specific criteria (Kriz, 2008), but is straightforward in method.

We adopt a debriefing approach in preference to using the score-based performance metrics generated automatically by the simulation game. A number of authors advise against using only performance metrics as measures for assessing learning and understanding, not least because it is often by making mistakes, then critically reflecting on those mistakes, that we learn. Indeed, studies have indicated that there is little or no correlation between game performance and learning (Gosen and Washbush, 2004; Anderson and Lawton, 2009 for the full argument).

Within the module, oral debriefing forms the primary basis for assessing the business knowledge and understanding that students have developed during the gaming experience. A role-play discussion with each team (or board of directors) is carried out over a 20–30 minute period. This discussion is summatively assessed (carrying a weighting of 30% of the final module mark).

Whilst oral debriefing is used for the assessment, it is preceded by a written debriefing. Petranek (2000) argues that a written debriefing of this kind helps to solidify the learning arising from the students' SG experience. The student teams prepare for oral debriefing by producing a short report, incorporating relevant information, models and graphics, which serves two purposes. Firstly, it forces the students to engage in a written debriefing exercise after gaming, thus helping to crystallise their thinking. Secondly, it provides instructors with the necessary evidence to steer a full oral discussion.

For the oral debriefing, each team remains in-role as company directors, and the two tutors adopt the role of fund managers exploring potential investment in each company. The discussion takes the form of a 'scripted role-play,' which helps structure the interaction between the different 'actors' within the role-play. The tutors question the team about aspects of their strategy and performance over the gaming rounds and ask them about the future direction and prospects of the company. The teams are probed on a wide range of issues pertaining to the running of the company, some general and some specific. Questions might relate to the past, present or future situation of the company. The questions are based on the ILOs for the module and used for measuring understanding of the following:

- the strategic planning process adopted
- implementation of strategy
- the influence of the macro and competitive environments on strategy making
- factors affecting company performance
- mistakes made and strategic lessons learned.

Students are awarded an overall group grade based on the following criteria:

- ability to articulate a clear vision and purpose
- ability to analyse their business environment (both internal and external)
- understanding of strategic options and reasoning behind their adopted strategy
- understanding of the link between strategy, decisions and outcomes
- understanding of team dynamic and performance
- ability to deal with probing questions and engage in dialogue.

Although an overall grade is awarded, it would be possible to individualise grades through supplementary learning journals or through a 360°-peer appraisal within each team. The latter may, for example, entail the award of an aggregate pool of marks to a team, which can then be divided and allocated by the team to the individual students, subject to agreement with the tutor.

Evaluation

There are a number of challenges inherent to this form of learning and assessment. First, the design and development of SG teaching and learning and associated assessment activities can be time and resource intensive. SGs are not self-teaching, and particular consideration needs to be given on how to integrate the gaming activity with other learning on the module.

Careful planning of the scripted role-play for the oral debriefing is needed to ensure that the assessment of the student experience is fit for purpose, fair to all, and consistent with measuring student attainment of ILOs. In the context of this part-time programme, students' opportunities to meet to work on the SG are constrained, due to both work commitments and the fact that they are geographically dispersed.

Hence, it is important to schedule instructor-supported computer laboratory sessions of sufficient timescale to allow students to work collaboratively on the web-based SG. This contrasts with full-time programmes, where it is often the case that students will schedule their own team meetings outside timetabled classes. The moderation of oral debriefing assessment requires some special preparation to ensure marking consistency. For this module, all debriefings are conducted by two tutors. In addition, all debriefings are video recorded and copies provided for external examining purposes.

Whilst these challenges exist, an evaluation of student feedback indicates a number of benefits associated with simulation gaming and oral debriefing. Students have indicated that the approach brought the theoretical aspects of the module to life, and that simulation gaming is particularly suited to postgraduate learners who are keen to apply theory in a real-world context. Students have also mentioned that the simulation gaming experience is distinctive, enjoyable and even addictive.

Discussion

Employing SGs in the classroom calls for an active and student-centred style of teaching. This in turn provides the opportunity to adopt assessment methods that differ from those more traditionally favoured on many business and management modules. Given the importance of reflection to the attainment of ILOs through simulation gaming, oral debriefing lends itself well to the assessment of student learning.

From the experience we have garnered from administering this type of assessment to postgraduate, post-experience learners, we would say that oral debriefing of simulation gaming brings particular benefits to this group, through higher levels of verisimilitude and context relevance. This could in part explain why student attainment on the module has been consistently high and often at distinction level.

The techniques we adopted align well with Kolb's (1984) Learning Cycle in that the approach enabled us to assess how students act in response to challenges within a sustained dynamic setting, how they reflect and learn from the consequences of their actions and how this informs fresh action. This also illustrates a general lesson we have learned from using oral debriefing: that it has a part to play in assessing and enhancing sets of skills and abilities that might not be so easily appraised through other assessment techniques.

References and URLs

Anderson, P. H. & Lawton, L. (1988) Assessing Student Performance on a Business Simulation Exercise. *Developments in Business Simulation & Experiential Learning* 15 pp. 241–45

Anderson, P. H. & Lawton, L. (2009) Business Simulations and Cognitive Learning: Developments, Desires, and Future Directions. *Simulation & Gaming* 40 (2) pp. 193–216

Edelheim, J. & Ueda, D. (2007) Effective Use of Simulations in Hospitality Management Education – a Case Study. *Journal of Hospitality, Leisure, Sport & Tourism Education* 6 (1) pp. 18–28

Garris, R., Ahlers, R. & Driskell, J. E. (2002) Games, Motivation, and Learning: A Research and Practice Model. *Simulation & Gaming* 33 (4) pp. 441–67

Gosen, J. & Washbush, J. (2004) A Review of Scholarship on Assessing Experiential Learning Effectiveness. *Simulation & Gaming* 35 (2) pp. 270–93

Knotts, U. S. & Keys, J. B. Teaching Strategic Management with a Business Game. *Simulation Gaming* 28 (4) pp. 377–94

Kolb, D. A. (1984) *Experiential Learning, Experience as a Source of Learning and Development.* NJ: Prentice-Hall

Kriz, W. C. (2008) A Systemic-Constructivist Approach to the Facilitation and Debriefing of Simulations and Games. *Simulation & Gaming OnlineFirst*, published on June 20, 2008 as doi:10.1177/1046878108319867

Moizer, J., Lean, J., Towler, M. & Smith G. (2006) Modes of Learning in the Use of a Computer-based Business Simulation Game. *International Journal of Learning Technology* 2 (1) pp. 49–60

Petranek, C. F. (2000) Written Debriefing: The Next Vital Step in Learning with Simulations. *Simulation & Gaming* 31 pp. 108–18

Sutcliffe, M. (2002) Games, Simulations and Role-playing. *The Handbook for Economics Lecturers.* Bristol: Economics LTSN

Thompson, A. A. Jr., Stappenbeck, G. J. & Reidenbach, M. A. (2009) *The Business Strategy Game: Competing in the Global Marketplace* (2009 ed) IL: Irwin McGraw-Hill

DR JONATHAN LEAN is a senior lecturer in strategic management. He has published widely in the field of small business training and development and is actively engaged in research relating to the teaching of business strategy using simulation games.

DR JONATHAN MOIZER is a lecturer in business operations and strategy. He has published a number of papers in peer-reviewed journals in the field of business simulation and gaming. Jonathan is a Fellow of the Higher Education Academy.

14

Assessment for learning
Active learning in live projects

Ursula S. Hummel
Heidelberg International Business Academy

This chapter makes the case for active learning through live projects to bring the real world into business management education and better prepare future leaders for the uncertain, complex world of rapid change outside the classroom. In this context, the focus of assessment is shifted from marking exercises to become a meaningful contribution to learning and personal development as students and tutors obtain feedback from the business world.

Introduction

Heidelberg International Business Academy (HIB) is a business school with an international study programme modelled on the UK system that leads to the degree-level award of Bachelor of Arts (Honours); it is also an associate institution of the Open University.

This chapter offers a review of recent literature about three forms of active learning: (1) simulated student projects are contrasted with live projects in the form of (2) internal service projects and (3) projects with external partners. Type (3) is referred to in the literature as *service learning* and student *consulting projects* (Eyler & Giles, 1999; Cooke & Williams, 2004). While most of the literature seems to focus on the effects of the students' personal development, this chapter discusses the relationship between motivation, assessment and role perceptions, and highlights the positive effects on aspects of student employability, as well as on the students' and lecturers' professionalism and identification with the institution.

Rationale

The literature on active learning focuses on the methodological side of the learning experience, that is, combining classroom-based theoretical learning and practical experience in order to drive personal development. Little importance has been given, however, to assessment strategies for 'live' or real world projects.

> For students, assessment standards provide guidance for their learning and allow them to monitor their progress, and ultimately, the standards will be used to judge their performance. Yet there has been little serious consideration of the nature of assessment standards or their effective communication between stakeholders

(primarily staff and students but also employers, professional bodies and government) (Price et al, 2008: 1).

Context

In this chapter we discuss three forms of bringing the real world into the classroom.

❏ **Internal service projects**
where the students' own academic community benefits from a service brought to the institution that previously did not exist.

❏ **Service-learning projects**
where the intended beneficiary is located outside the academic community. Although service learning is defined in various ways in the literature, it is widely recognised as an educational approach that combines a service project for an organisation in the community (the service) with theoretical academic education (the learning). Most authors point out that service learning is distinguished by reflection and in-depth integration of theory and practice. The 'live' project provides sustainable real learning, plus the experience of work, and a contribution to a sense of civic responsibility (Eyler & Giles, 1999; Sliwka, 2006; Bartsch, 2009).

❏ **Student consulting projects**
which require students to work through business problems and to interact with working professionals.

Client projects – whether they are completed through a formal academic consultancy service or through an informal consultancy service represented by a classroom project – strengthen our profession by facilitating communication between academia and businesses. Professionals shape the education of future graduates, students gain practical experience that surpasses any classroom simulation or case study, and teachers remain in touch with business trends and practices (Cooke & Williams, 2004: 150).

The study took place at the Heidelberg International Business Academy (HIB); 280 students and five lecturers were involved. The Level 5 core module *Project Management and Professional Communication* was the appropriate course in which to run the project.

Learning outcomes and assessment method

To pass the module, students are expected to demonstrate in-depth understanding of project management and communication requirements in typical business situations and to develop entrepreneurial thinking. Moreover, they are expected to improve their time management, team-working and analytical skills. The following methods of summative assessment were used:

❏ A group report documenting the project management process, project objectives, stakeholder expectations, scheduling and project performance.

❏ A group or individual presentation of the project to HIB-internal stake holders and/or project partners.

❏ An individual reflective logbook documenting the student's own contribution to the project success and achievement of module learning outcomes.

Table 1 provides an overview of the module organisation and the alignment of teaching, learning, practical experience, reflection and assessment.

Table 1   Learning, teaching & assessment

Learning format and experience	Learning & teaching methods and forms	Student and tutor involvement	Assessment element(s)
Lectures: academic learning experience	Project management and business communication theory	Student-centred, but tutor-led sessions, supported by literature and virtual learning environment	Final project report (summative, 34% of the final mark)
			Final project presentation (summative, 33% of the final mark)
Reflective sessions: integration of theory and practice	Students reflect on and exchange the experience in their live projects.	Round-table discussions; the tutors normally introduce this format, give recommendations and a set of questions.	Informal but structured reflection (formative)
			Student logbook (summative, 33% of the final mark)
External partner involvement: practical learning experience	Meetings/presentations	Project teams present and discuss their project tasks to and with the external partner	Tutor feedback – debriefing of the meeting (formative)
	Business communication	Phone calls, emails, letters, presentations	Tutor feedback (formative)

Case study methodology

The current research took place within the Heidelberg International Business Academy between September 2007 and May 2010.

Phase 1

In the first phase, from September 2007 to May 2008, most projects were conducted as **simulations**.

Phase 2

In phase 2, there was a clear shift from simulated to **live projects**. Between September 2008 and May 2009, all students were involved in 'real world', live projects.

Phase 3

In phase 3, starting in September 2009 and lasting until May 2010, all students were involved in live **service or consultancy projects** with external partners.

There were three primary research questions:

❏ What were the students' perceptions regarding their motivation and role in order to bring their project to a team success?

❏ What were the students' perceptions regarding their own learning and personal development? and finally,

❑ How has assessment contributed to enhanced learning in view of the desired outcome of reflective managers?

Case study phase 1: Simulated projects and internal service projects

Between September 2007 and May 2008, 120 Level 5 students were involved in the design and planning of ten simulated and two internal service projects (project teams). Table 2 shows two typical project examples:

Table 2   Simulated and internal service project examples (Phase 1)

Project	Academic topic(s)	Brief description
A marketing study for the Pro-A league basketball club USC Heidelberg – a project simulation	Target groups analysis SWOT-analysis Marketing communication, i.e. advertising, posters, etc.	Students analysed the then situation of the club, its published goals to increase the number of spectators per match, and developed a marketing strategy.
The guide for new HIB students – an internal service project	Brochure design Budgeting Fundraising Business communication	Students developed a brochure for new and prospective HIB students containing relevant information for their study programme and practical advice for student life in Heidelberg.

Assessment method

Students had to hand in a group report and give an individual presentation about their project in front of level 4 HIB students (each element carrying 50% of the module mark). The quality of the project reports and presentations indicated that all projects had addressed the learning outcome for the students demonstrating an understanding of project management techniques.

Only one student team (representing eight per cent of the cohort) was able to link project management to strategic thinking and there was no evidence of entrepreneurial thinking. Another area of weaknesses concerned key transferable skills: the quality of most project budgets and schedules indicated that the assessment requirements did not encourage the students to focus enough on the development of analytical skills.

The gap identified in the alignment of assessment and learning outcomes was also reflected by the students' motivation. Feedback questionnaires showed the two extremes reflected in the split of marks. All students in the 'Guide for new HIB students' project (which achieved the best mark) noted 'deep understanding of communication, project management and fundraising techniques' and 'a wonderful team experience and feeling of satisfaction when we held the printed guide in our hands'. More than 65% of the students in the simulated projects, however, reported 'difficult periods in our teams when we learned that we could not realise our projects but had to run them as a simulation' and 'it was difficult to stay motivated'. A minority (6%) of the students even noted 'a complete lack of motivation to work on a project which is just a simulation'.

Case study phases 2 and 3: Live projects

From September 2008 and up to the time of writing in early 2010, all Level 5 HIB students (approximately 160 so far) have been involved in live projects. Table 3 shows two project examples from phase 2.

Table 3: Live project examples (Phase 2)

Project	Academic topic(s)	Brief description
¡Caramba! A guide to Spanish life in the Rhein-Neckar metropolitan region – a service project	Identifying target groups Brochure design Budgeting Fundraising Event management Marketing communication with a focus on media articles	*¡Caramba!* is a brochure about Spanish culture in the region, released to promote an event called *Día hispánico*, a Spanish day with typical food and drinks, music, workshops and lectures.
'Vote them big' A newcomer band contest for BigFM – a service project in co-operation with a major German radio chain	Identifying target groups and newcomer bands Event design/management Marketing communication Event promotion Advertising Business communication	Students first identified suitable newcomer bands and studied the typical target groups of BigFM. In a web-based pre-contest, the bands for the final contest, which students helped to put into action, were selected.

The assessment method of this phase remained unchanged but, following an review of assessment design in phase 1, all project reports now had to be evaluated by the external partners and internal stakeholders, with a focus on project budgets, marketing objectives and team performance. Students documented the quantitative and qualitative results of these evaluations and included their reflections in the final report. Comparing the assessment tasks of both phases, two significant improvements can be observed:

❏ the marks achieved showed on average an improvement of 0.3%
❏ students demonstrated much better analytical and time management skills.

It became clear that the assessed transferable skill of reflection and analysis had improved the students' ability to understand the strategic relevance of project management.

Student feedback

Student feedback indicated that there was a clear increase in their motivation. Over 80% of the students recognised that they 'learned a lot and had so much fun together' and 'managed to overcome even difficult periods. At the end we were a real team.' However, the student group organising the Spanish Day (12% of the cohort) noted it felt great to stand in front of all the students and guests and tell them about our project. But after the *Día hispánico*, we were so tired, we could not bring ourselves to prepare for the next assessments. In the end, some of our results in other modules suffered.

Assessment method and design in phase 3

Based on the improvements in phase 2 and since student feedback also clearly asked that individual students' contributions to the project be recognised, a stronger focus on reflection seemed most appropriate to improve the students' learning experience. As of phase 3, there are three summative assessment elements, each one weighing one third of the final mark:

❑ **A group project report**

After feedback from the module tutor, this report is handed over to the external project partner. Students see this as a difficult (but motivating) extra challenge, as some project partners are potential future employers.

❑ **An individual presentation**

Students present their project in front of a mixed group of other students and lecturers and/or external partners. Apart from their relevance for summative assessment, these presentations also serve the purpose of internal dissemination and good performances can motivate and inspire other students. In presentations to external partners, students get a chance to display their presentation skills to the professionals, which challenges and motivates them at the same time.

❑ An individual student log-book

Students document their individual role and tasks in the project, write a reflective report about it, and assess the quality of their own contribution. Student self-assessment and the tutor's assessment of the reflective reports each count 50% of the mark. Students seem to understand the relevance of this assessment element for their own professional development.

Table 4 presents two examples of projects in phase 3, the first shows Heidelberg as a tourist destination for disabled travellers, and the second a fundraising strategy:

Evaluation

Assessment for learning

Brown et al (1997) point out on the relevance of assessment for student learning:

Assessment defines what students regard as important, how they spend their time and how they come to see themselves as students and then as graduates. If you want to change student learning then change the methods of assessment.

Students were asked which forms of assessment made a difference in their perceptions of their own learning. In phase 1, students seemed to focus exclusively on the final project report. Some of them regarded reflection on the simulated projects as

Table 4   Service learning and student consulting projects (Phase 3)

Project	Academic topic(s)	Brief description
Heidelberg: A tourist destination without barriers – a consultancy project for Heidelberg Marketing GmbH	Target group analysis Destination analysis Tourism management Design of tourism offers including booking tools Marketing communication with a special focus on web site management	Elderly people and travellers with reduced mobility (e.g. tourists in wheel-chairs) are identified as a target group of growing importance. In this project students analyse the state-of-the-art for disabled tourists, evaluate Heidelberg as a suitable destination and develop three 2–3 day bookable tourism offers.
'Lesedi Show Choir': An fundraising strategy for a South African choir in Heidelberg/ZA – a service project in co-operation with a cultural and festival organisation in Heidelberg (Germany)	Fundraising Marketing communication with a focus on web design and website management Aspects of cultural management Business communication mainly with potential sponsors	In this social and cultural project with an international dimension, students design and implement a fundraising strategy aimed at raising enough money for the 'Lesedi Show Choir' to participate in the music festival *Heidelberger Frühling*.

a rather useless time-wasting experience. Both tutor observations and student comments strengthen the project teams' commitment to the success of their project and the quality of the final report. All students stated that they perceived feedback on the final project report to be more meaningful when the report had been written not 'just' for a mark, but as documentation for the external partner.

All students who had the opportunity to present their project in front of external partners said that they were very proud of what they had achieved, and it helped them in their personal development to get feedback from industry professionals. It goes without saying that this aspect is not only vital for the students' perception of their own learning, but also for the tutors to stay in touch with the standards of the professional world.

> Service learning has the potential to transform business undergraduate education. Service learning affects major areas such as theory-to-real-world linkage, ability to change with the environment, and capacity to foster innovation. These areas prepare students for post-graduate programmes and future careers (Govenar & Rikshi, 2007: 9)

Role perceptions

Price et al postulate in their six tenets for changed assessment standards:

> When it comes to the assessment of learning, we need to move beyond systems focused on marks and grades towards the valid assessment of the achievement of intended programme outcomes.' (2008: 2).

Student and tutor comments on live projects clearly indicate that the parameters for achievement go beyond the traditional student and tutor role perceptions. Projects that included an event were perceived to be successful or not – regardless of the mark given to assessment elements – according to the number of visitors who came. All projects were ultimately measured according to their financial performance. Thus students have a chance to experience real-world behaviour and academic teachers can focus on their task as facilitators of learning.

Discussion and conclusion

Lessons for academic staff

This study clearly indicates the benefits of live projects over simulations for both students and staff. In successful live projects, the most valuable learning experience is driven by the achievement of goals – like in the real world of business.

> Business management courses teach that the formulation of objectives on both organisational and individual levels is a precursor for achievement of desired business outcomes' (Steiner & Watson, 2008: 422).

However, not every team will achieve its goals. Therefore, it is the role of the module tutor to balance any negative real-world experiences, typically due to a mis-match of initial project objectives and actual achievement. To mention an example, students in the fundraising project 'Lesedi Show Choir' got rather frustrated by the low response rate to letters they had sent to companies asking for a contribution. In a reflective session with the module tutor and the external partner following the campaign, they were able to analyse the reasons for their lack of success and develop an improved communication strategy.

Students need to develop the capacity to monitor the quality of their own work. Self-assessment is a skill to be learned. It is necessary for further academic study and it is critical to all of the students' future work and to their careers. Real projects can wean students away from depending on tutor feedback and can help to create an appreciation of how to improve time spent in the workplace. In project teams students learn from each other and apply the increased knowledge to their own work. (Learning and remembering content is most effective when it is taught to somebody else).

Enhanced student learning through assessment

This case study shows that learning in live projects is best when:

❑ Assessment combines individual and group tasks which are linked to systematic reflection.

❑ Students understand the assessment elements not just as an exercise to achieve a mark for the module, but as a piece of work which is presented internally and to the business world.

❑ Feedback is given in a real life context, where students are not the only ones being assessed, as both students and tutors represent the academic community in front of business partners.

Students seem to be more open to reflective practice once they have understood that reflection is a meta-cognitive skill which lays the foundation for independent and life-long learning. This shift in perceptions is supported once the traditional student and tutor roles are changed. As Bartsch points out, most managers have not learned to reflect on their own behaviour in a systematic meaningful way. Today's leaders typically cannot describe and reflect on why and how they took which decisions. But the meta-cognitive skill of self-evaluation is crucial in the complex business world. Self-reflection is a core competence for ethical business behaviour (2009: 109). Business schools which are committed to preparing managers for tomorrow's business world should pay special attention to meta-cognitive abilities.

References

Bartsch, G. (2009) Service Learning im Kontext von Zivilgesellschaft. In Altschmidt, K., Miller, J. and Stark, W. eds. (2009) *Raus aus dem Elfenbeinturm? Entwicklungen in Service Learning und bürgerschaftlichem Engagement an deutschen Hochschulen*. Weinheim und Basel: Beltz-Verlag pp. 102–9

Brown, G., Bull, J. and Pendlebury, M. (1997) *Assessing Student Learning in Higher Education*. London: Routledge

Cooke, L. and Williams, S. (2004) Two Approaches to Using Client Projects in the College Classroom. *Business Communication Quarterly* 67 (2) pp. 139–52

Eyler, J. and Giles, D. (1999) *Where's the learning in service-learning?* San Francisco: Jossey-Bass

Govekar, M. and Rishi, M. (2007) Service Learning: Bringing Real-World Education Into the B-School Classroom. *Journal of Education for Business* September/October pp 3–10

Price, M., O'Donovan, B., Rust, C. and Carroll, J. (2008) Assessment Standards. A Manifesto for Change. *The Brookes eJournal of Learning and Teaching* 2 (3) pp 1–8

Sliwka, A. (2006) Reflexion als zentrale Komponente des Service Learning, Vortrag [Web Source] From www.servicelearning.de/fileadmin/user_upload/dokumente/Vortrag_Service_Learning_Reflexion _Mai_2006.pdf [accessed 18.11.09]

Steiner, S. and Watson, M. (2008) The Service Learning Component in Business Education: The Values Linkage Void. *Academy of Management Learning & Education* 5 (4) pp. 422–34

URSULA S. HUMMEL is a senior lecturer in project, communication and service management at Heidelberg International Business Academy (HIB). She completed her MA in linguistics at the University of Constance in 1983 and her State Exam in teaching at the University of Heidelberg in 1986. After completing postgraduate business and marketing studies at the Bad Harzburg Business Academy she worked as an international sales manager in the packaging industry, and has been a member of HIB's permanent teaching staff for the last ten years. Her current research interests include teaching pedagogy in business education as well as the linkage of higher education institutions with the surrounding community and the real world of business.

15

Programme-led assessment strategies in sports development degrees

Linda Allin and Lesley Fishwick
Northumbria University

This chapter explains how a programme-led approach was adopted within a BA (Hons) Sports Development with Coaching degree. Key examples of success factors for Assessment for Learning (AfL) are highlighted, including engaging students in assessment processes and the impact on student learning.

Context and rationale

In 2005, Northumbria University was awarded a Centre of Excellence for Learning (CETL), specifically for Assessment for Learning. The university Teaching and Learning Strategy 2007–10 includes developing assessment as a tool for effective learning as a key area of that strategy area. One strategic objective for the university is to 'operationalise the six CETL Assessment for Learning criteria in all programmes'.

The CETL in Assessment for Learning at Northumbria University (www.northumbria.ac.uk/cetl–afl/), proposes six conditions for the support of AfL, which are developed through a learning environment that:

❏ Emphasises authenticity and complexity in the content and methods of assessment rather than reproduction of knowledge and reductive measurement.
❏ Uses high-stakes summative assessment rigorously, but sparingly, rather than as the main driver for learning.
❏ Offers students extensive opportunities to engage in the kinds of tasks that develop and demonstrate their learning, thus building their confidence and capabilities before they are summatively assessed.
❏ Is rich in feedback derived from formal mechanisms e.g. tutor comments on assignments, student self-review logs.
❏ Is rich in informal feedback (for example, peer review of draft writing, collaborative project work) which provides students with a continuous flow of feedback on 'how they are doing'.
❏ Develops students' abilities to direct their own learning, evaluate their own progress and attainments and support the learning of others.

The case study examines these six criteria and shows how the CETL plays a large part in working with university schools and divisions to embed AfL. It explains how members of staff within the Division of Sport Sciences have become affiliated to the CETL (AfL) as CETL associates, and are working with the CETL to further develop excellence in teaching and learning within the Division. At the heart of our approach to embedding AfL across the degree programme is a clear academic rationale based on assessment for learning principles. The case study outlines our commitment to developing assessment procedures that address factors that contribute to learning and help build an individual's enthusiasm for learning (Broadfoot, 2008).

The BA (Hons) Sports Development with Coaching programme is a significant part of the sport undergraduate portfolio at Northumbria University. There are approximately 70 students per year on this programme, which includes core modules such as *Managing and Developing Sport; Sport in Society; Community Sports Development; Strategic and Development Planning in Sport; Sport Organisations: Policy to Practice;* and *Sports Equity.* Students also undertake a work placement in the second year, and can opt to take a *Professional Development through Sport* module which provides further placement learning and assessment in their final year. The case study details the main features of our AfL approach adopted through this programme over the course of 18 months.

Description

Investigating staff understanding of AfL and assessment processes

One of the first elements in the process of embedding AfL was to explore the current knowledge and understanding of sport staff. A small team of CETL associates in sport worked together to devise an interview schedule to probe staff views of assessment, their knowledge of formative assessment, and their current assessment practices, at the same time identifying any barriers or issues which stood in the way of them setting their 'ideal assessment' for students in their specific sport modules. A research assistant was employed to undertake semi-structured interviews, which were then transcribed, anonymised, and returned to the CETL team for analysis. The initial findings from this study were then fed back to staff. An important part of this initial process was to gain staff trust in the CETL team and to see their approach as a focus on enhancement of the assessment process rather than as a quality-assurance mechanism.

Implementing initial staff workshops and learning teaching and assessment (LTA) forums

Following the research into staff knowledge and understanding of assessment for learning, a series of staff workshops were delivered by sport CETL associates and a learning and teaching advisor. The workshops centred on explaining assessment for learning, giving examples of good and innovative practice in sports development, and responding to staff queries as to how to develop innovative assessment for learning practices within a context of widening participation and increasing numbers of students on sports courses. Learning, Teaching and Assessment (LTA) Forums were established within the division to occur twice per semester for all staff. These forums were on a range of topics and included staff development on providing feedback, marking consistency and innovative assessment practices.

Involving students in assessments

An important element of our strategy of moving towards more student-centred assessment was to involve students in the assessment process. Student representatives in their final year were invited to review a number of assessment outlines and marking criteria for sport modules. They were asked to make comments on the clarity and learning value of the assessment from a student perspective. Student comments were then fed into the next assessment panel process within the division. The assessment panel is an internal process which evaluates staff assessments before they are sent to external examiners. The panel pays attention to the level, consistency and clarity of assessment across the programme, and makes recommendations for change where appropriate.

To further engage students in assessment processes, staff were encouraged to involve students in 'assessment dialogues' within their specific modules. This was to facilitate shared understandings between tutors and students regarding the nature of the assessment (Carless, 2006).

Away day to discuss programme assessment strategies

A staff away day was held at the end of the academic year 2007–08. This was an opportunity to highlight the importance of a programme level approach and share experiences. Staff programme teams were invited to audit their current practices and were given time and space to discuss and review their programme assessment strategies in relation to assessment for learning. This also involved a mapping exercise of module assessments and outcomes against the programme learning outcomes (both skills and content based). Programme leaders took notes from these meetings to be followed up in programme team discussions in 2008–09.

Assessment changes in relation to a new academic calendar

During the academic year 2008–09, the university made the decision to amend the academic calendar for 2009–10 towards two 13-week semesters, an earlier start in January and an identified assessment period for three weeks after Easter. Part of the aim of the calendar change was to reduce the number of examinations held in January, and to be more flexible in assessment approaches. The change in the academic calendar was timely, in that it followed the assessment discussions in the division. Unlike other divisions, we were prepared and in a positive frame of mind to be making changes to assessment. A management team meeting was held to identify a timetable for changes, and to include time for further programme levels discussions as well as administrative deadlines for module changes.

Identification of formative assessment strategies in all assessment outlines to students

The university teaching and learning strategy included asking staff to identify their formative assessment practices in module descriptors. Within sport, staff were asked to incorporate both formative and summative assessment into their module assessment briefs to be distributed to students at the beginning of the semester. In this way, the role of feedback as a way of enabling feed-forward (Duncan, 2007) to future tasks was to become explicit in student documentation. Staff were encouraged to identify tutor and peer feedback opportunities, both written and oral.

Evaluation

Modules incorporating AfL

Table 1 provides an indication of how AfL principles were incorporated into specific modules across the *Sports Development with Coaching* programme. Module tutors were requested to engage the students in formative feedback. This was important both

Table 1   AfL approaches in sports development with coaching modules

Assessment Type	Level	Feedback Mode		
		Self	Peer	Tutor
MCQ examination *Sport and Social Issues*	4	*		*
Media headlines portfolio *Sport and Social issues*	4	*	*	
Reflective log *Personal Skills Development*	4	*	*	*
Mind map *Managing and Developing Sport*	4		*	*
Action-research group project *Community Sports Development*	5	*	*	*
Work placement portfolio *Sports Development Placement*	5	*		*
Lesson plans *Coaching Behaviours*	5	*		*
Video coaching session *Applied Coaching Practice*	6	*	*	*
Poster *Sport on the Cultural Agenda*	6		*	*
Awareness reflective portfolio *Sport Equity*	6	*		*

when introducing new assessment methods and where assessment modes remained quite traditional. For example, where a more traditional multiple-choice question (MCQ) examination was used as a summative assessment, the module leader facilitated a formative assessment session where students designed questions, held a quiz and discussed both answers and questions.

For a more innovative approach, a take-home exam assessment, the module tutor held assessment workshops on a mock exam earlier in the semester. This allowed the students a variety of opportunities for feedback on tasks that helped develop their learning. Types of feedback used within these formative processes are also indicated in Table 1. For further discussion of the engagement with formative feedback refer to Fishwick and Allin, (2009).

In general, the module assessments received favourable comments from external examiners. In relation to the overall programme, the external examiner for the *Sports Development with Coaching* programme made specific reference to the innovative and authentic assessment practices evident within the programme and commented that 'the range of assessment methods employed is impressive, and there are some imaginative and interesting coursework tasks'.

Student engagement with AfL

In the first year of adoption of AfL, module reviews suggested that students were largely satisfied with the module-assessment processes. For example, over 85% of students provided 'agreed' or 'strongly agreed' responses to questions relating to the learning and teaching approaches, learning materials, taught sessions, module support, staff accessibility and formative feedback helping them learn in the *Community Sports Development* module. This module's summative assessment required the students to engage with outside agencies and organisations to complete a small-scale action-research evaluation project and a series of formative assessment workshops were devised to lead them through this process. Almost 95% of students agreed or strongly agreed that the assessment methods used related well to the content and learning outcomes. The module was further evaluated by a focus group and students highlighted the relevance and authenticity of the assessment in terms of having to complete research in the 'real world'. One student commented

the difference is though, this module is a lot more practical; the last time we were just given a question and given the results and we had to write the discussion, whereas this time we've actually gone out and done it and understand much more about the question.

Another student emphasised the real world nature of the assessment

you've got all your theory-based knowledge from your lectures, you can actually apply that to the real world, but then you can draw on that real world experience in other theories, you can make it into something rather than a textbook in front of you.

Overall, the students highly valued the module in terms of the student-centred learning and rated it as invaluable preparation for their dissertation.

In the module *Sport on the Cultural Agenda*, the summative assessment was new and took the form of a take-home exam made up of three questions. To prepare for this the students were set an independent study task in the form of a mock take-home exam. The question format mirrored the actual exam, ranging from definitions, to theoretical analysis, to application to practice. A discussion board was set up and a specific assessment workshop held which involved peer, self and tutor marking and feedback. The mock-exam exercise was fully evaluated using questionnaires and a focus group interview. The students indicated that the mock exam had been challenging and had encouraged them to delve more deeply into the readings.

The students also highlighted that they had developed a much clearer idea of the expectations and requirements for the summative assessment and indicated that the workshop had both motivated them and reassured them about the assessment. The level of engagement with the task of the 30 students was very high, as the discussion board had over 122 threads of discussion, several of which were visited over 50 times. Overall, the results of the evaluation indicated that the students valued highly this different approach to assessment and the opportunity for them to be engaged in assessment dialogues (Black and Wiliam, 1998; Rust, O'Donovan and Price, 2003).

Staff engagement with AfL

Reflections from programme teams, module tutors and the CETL sport team indicate that there was a noticeable shift in terms of the willingness of staff to discuss assessment more openly with each other, and with students. A multi-pronged approach encouraged active engagement of sport staff in assessment for learning via learning, teaching and assessment (LTA) forums, programme meetings and an assessment panel. LTA forums facilitated open discussion about assessment and offered an opportunity to share examples of innovative assessment practices. There was a consensus in the Sport division that assessment is not just about the grade but about the process of learning. Additionally, there is an appreciation that the processes of feedback and feed-forward are essential elements for engaging students in assessment dialogues. Staff continue to express some concerns at the increasing numbers of students who arrive at university as seemingly dependent learners. Staff identified the need to try different pedagogic approaches to engage students and foster independent learning.

Key features for success

Listed below are the reflections of the authors on the key features of the approach which enabled the successful incorporation of AfL into the programme:

❑ Bottom-up approach to gain buy-in from staff
   The LTA forums and interactive discussions about good practice gave the staff many opportunities to feed into the process of assessment changes.

❑ Discussions and ownership within programme teams

The programme-level discussions allowed staff to see to more clearly how their own assessment requirements fitted into the overall programme strategy. This facilitated discussions on the sequencing and progression of assessments across levels and led to the use of a much greater variety of assessment methods across programmes.

❑ Enthusiasm of CETL associates

The presence of CETL associates within the programme team generated an enthusiasm and an expertise about assessment. This in turn encouraged the staff to ask questions and stimulate discussions about assessment practices.

❑ Assessment panel with clear guidelines

The clear guidelines set out by the assessment panel and peer review of assessment briefs across the programme improved both the standardisation in terms of requirements within levels of study and the clarity of given tasks.

❑ Buy-in from students regarding the relevance of assessments

Involving the students in the reviewing of assessment criteria, and also increasing the opportunities for assessment dialogues between staff and students, clarified expectations across levels.

❑ Support available from CETL and CETL associates

The resources available at CETL and the opportunities to discuss assessment issues with like-minded individuals created a vibrant assessment culture within the programme team.

❑ Designing innovative assessments for large cohorts without overburdening staff

Recognition of the time pressures and potential burden on staff of increasing student numbers led to discussions focused on potential solutions in terms of alternative and innovative assessments.

❑ Sharing good practice

The willingness to share ideas and examples of what worked and the provision of space and time in terms of the LTA forums was a lynchpin in this approach at a programme level.

Discussion: challenges and lessons learned

The success of embedding AfL into the sport programme was not without its challenges. These included the time pressures on academic staff as well as more subtle aspects, such as initial resistance to change traditional assessment modes and uncertainty of academic calendar changes during the process. Staff were understandably concerned about the impact that changes would have on workload and the implications for marking, particularly when traditional examination formats were being exchanged for more authentic assessments. They were also concerned that, whilst creative assessment changes might be supported in the informal process, they might be challenged within the more formal divisional assessment panel. Moreover, the processes for assessment change within the school meant that any changes to assessment type or format within a module descriptor involved the completion and submission of forms to a quality sub-committee.

It was therefore important for the programme director to work with the associate dean for teaching and learning in the school, to ensure that new assessments could be managed practically within quality-assurance frameworks. For example, moving to multiple, in-class assessments with subsequent feedback, rather than one end of semester exam, required prior thought about timetabling, the potential use of computers versus paper-based tests, and how different seminar groups would be managed. Integrating a mind map into the *Sport Development* module required consideration of staff training on mind mapping and discussion with members of the assessment panel on equivalence in terms of word length policies for modules at the same level. It was also agreed with the associate dean that, for this period of change, changes in assessment dates could be handled at the divisional level, with minimum bureaucracy. Through all this, the challenge was to ensure a consistent message: that there was support for staff to be creative and take risks in assessment enhancements.

A key lesson learned was to ensure specific action plans were identified after useful programme discussions. It was easy to engage in discussions during an away day, for example, but then the momentum would be lost when notes were not detailed and not followed up immediately staff returned after the summer. It was also important to plan meetings around key dates for programme changes, which sometimes required meeting at difficult times. There remained ongoing challenges in reducing the workload involved in change and working within university administrative deadlines in order for changes to be implemented the following year.

Overall, the process was a successful one in developing understanding of assessment for learning with the sport division and implementing this at a programme level. One measure of success has been the number of staff having informal discussions about assessment in the corridors, and sharing their thoughts in general conversations or in other staff offices. Success in terms of student learning has been shown through student satisfaction with assessments and there has been the beginning of a cultural shift in terms of the move to more student-centred approaches and students engaging in assessment dialogues. However, it is important to recognise that this initial process of change marks the beginning of a much longer-term process of enhancing assessment within sport. Opportunities for staff development, assessment workshops, sharing of good practice and programme reviews need to continue if the embedding of AfL at the programme level is to be sustained.

References

Black, P. and Wiliam, D. (1998) Inside the black box: Raising standards through classroom assessment. *Phi Delta Kappan* **80** (2) pp. 1–12

Broadfoot, P. (2008) Assessment for learners: assessment literacy and the development of learning power. In A. Haynes and L. McDowell (eds) *Balancing Dilemmas in Assessment and Learning in Contemporary Education* Routledge pp. 213–24

Carless, D. (2006) Differing perceptions in the feedback process. *Studies in Higher Education* **31** (2) pp. 219–33

Duncan, N. (2007) 'Feed-forward': Improving students' use of tutor comments. *Assessment and Evaluation in Higher Education* **32** (3) pp. 271–83

Fishwick, L. and Allin, L. (2009) *HLST Engaging Sport Students in Assessment and Formative Feedback*. Subject Specific Guide. Available at http://www.heacademy.ac.uk/assets/hlst/documents/resources/ssg_allin_assessment_feedback.pdf (date accessed 15 September 2009)

O'Donovan, B., Price, M. and Rust, C. (2004) 'Know what I mean?' Enhancing student understanding of assessment standards and criteria'. *Teaching in Higher Education* **9** (3) pp. 325–35

Rust, C., O'Donovan, B. and Price, M. (2003) Improving students' learning by developing their understanding of assessment criteria and processes. *Assessment and Evaluation in Higher Education* **28** (2) pp. 147–64

LINDA ALLIN is Director of Quality Enhancement and a University Teaching Fellow in the Division of Sport Sciences at Northumbria University. Her subject specific teaching and research interests lie in sports development and coaching, with a specific focus on community sports development. She is co-author of the *Journal of Adventure Education and Outdoor Learning*. Linda is a CETL associate with the Centre for Excellence in Assessment for Learning and encourages and engages in pedagogic research through the Sport Learning and Teaching Research Unit (SPLaTR). Projects include student views of assessment and feedback, engaging employers, and student use of e-learning.

LESLEY FISHWICK is a Principal Lecturer, Teaching Fellow and CETL associate at Northumbria University. Her research interests have been in the broad area of sociology of sport, in particular women and sport, sporting identities and the social construction of healthy bodies. Her teaching fellowship scholarship focuses on a series of projects with SPLaTR (Sport, Learning and Teaching Research group) developing research innovation and enhancement in learning and teaching in sport-related fields. Areas of expertise include assessment and feedback, student engagement and the student learning experience.

The authors would like to thank the staff of the Division of Sport Sciences for their contributions in the development of programme assessment, and especially those who provided us with examples of assessment practices.

Glossary

AfL	Assessment for Learning
ASKe	Assessment Standards Knowledge exchange
AUQA	Australian Universities Quality Agency
BMAF	Higher Education Academy subject centre for business, management, accountancy and finance
BSG	business simulation games, *The Business Strategy Game* by Thompson et al (2009)
CAP	Centre of Academic Practice (QMU)
CETL	Centre for Excellence in Teaching and Learning
CoP	community of practice
CSS	Cardiff School of Sport (UWIC)
DMS	Diploma in Management Studies
FDTL	Fund for the Development of Learning and Teaching
GDP	Graduate Development Programme (University of the West of England)
HEFCE	Higher Education Funding Council
HEI	higher education institutions
HIB	Heidelberg International Business Academy
HLST	Higher Education Academy subject centre for hospitality, leisure, sport and tourism
ICT	information communication technologies
ILO	intended learning outcome
ISLE	Individualised Support for Learning through e-Portfolios
LJMU	Liverpool John Moores University
LTA	learning, teaching and assessment
MCQ	multiple-choice question examination
MOB	*Management and Organisational Behaviour* (MOB) module (University of the West of England)
MBTI	Myers-Briggs type indicator
OBU	Oxford Brookes University
ODL	open and distance learning
OSCE	objective structured clinical examinations
OU	the Open University
PAL	peer assisted learning

PBS	University of Plymouth Business School
PDP	personal development planning
QAA	Quality Assurance Agency for higher education
QMU	Queen Margaret University, Edinburgh
SD	standard deviation
SG	(business) simulation games
SFC	Scottish Funding Council
SPACE	Student-Staff Partnership for Assessment Change and Evaluation
SPLaTR	Sport Learning and Teaching Research Unit
SPSS	Statistical Package for Social Sciences
TLC	Towards Inclusive Assessment: Unleashing Creativity (Southampton Solent University)
USEM	Undestanding, Skills, Employability, Metacognition model (Yorke & Knight, 2006)
UWIC	University of Wales Institute Cardiff

Index

Forthcoming in Summer 2011

Enhancing Graduate Impact

in Business and Management Hospitality Leisure Sport and Tourism

Edited by Patsy Kemp and Richard Atfield

The fifth in the series of books commissioned by the Higher Education Academy subject centres for Hospitality, Leisure, Sport and Tourism (HLST) and Business, Management, Accountancy and Finance (BMAF), this publication will offer case studies containing approaches aimed at enabling students to become 'graduates with impact', a key priority of the Higher Education Academy.

See overleaf for the other titles in this highly successful series.

Other resources available from HLST and BMAF include the online journals JoHLSTE (Journal of Hospitality, Leisure, Sport and Tourism Education) and IJME (International Journal of Management Education) and the publications LINK and BMAF magazine.

For more information on these, and on the many other resources for assessment, learning and teaching in higher education, see http://www.heacademy.ac.uk/hlst/ and http://www.heacademy.ac.uk/business/.

£25.00 (paperback)	234 x 156mm	2011	176 pp	ISBN 978–1–903152–29–4

Enhancing the International Learning Experience

in Business and Management Hospitality Leisure Sport and Tourism

Edited by Richard Atfield and Patsy Kemp

Internationalisation is particularly pertinent for academic communities in the UK and around the world. Chapters range from implementing university-wide 'global perspectives' and assessment strategy through inter-university collaboration and review of programmes to the practicalities of adapting individual modules and developing specific learning activities.

Written by academics involved in international learning and teaching, the chapters offer insight into the successes and the pitfalls of embedding internationalisation into the learning experience for business, hospitality, leisure, sport and tourism students.

Contents

Contributors   Jan Bamford Nina Becket Maureen Brookes Jude Carroll Alan Darricotte Judie Gannon Rong Huang Elspeth Jones Patsy Kemp Sandra King Mike Lowe Jacqueline Lynch Rod McColl Mari Jo Pesch Sandie Randall Malcolm Sullivan Angela Vickerstaff Philip Warwick Melanie Weaver Rachel Wicaksono

£25.00 (paperback)   234 x 156mm   2008   176 pp   ISBN 978–1–903152–23–2

Enhancing
Student-centred Learning

in Business and Management Hospitality Leisure Sport and Tourism

Edited by John Buswell and Nina Becket

Outlines successful approaches in supporting the enhancement of student-centred learning. It embraces the theme of employability covered in the first book in this series and moves on to consider the importance of lifelong learning and the role of higher education in the development of independent, autonomous and self-empowered learners.

The case studies, written by academics, offer a variety of perspectives on student-centred learningwhile discussing lessons learned along the way. Each case study describes a practice or intervention which sets out to engage students and encourage them to take more responsibility for their learning.

Contents

Contributors Mark Atlay Graham Baker Colin Beard Wendy Beekes Karen Bill Will Bowen Jones Derry Corey Simon Cox Crispin Dale Robert French Louise Grisoni Jacqui Gush Carol Jarvis Christine Keenan Susan Lea Jacqueline Lynch Pru Marriot Dominic Micklewright Mark Moss Sarah Nixon Margaret Page Petia Petrova Peter Robinson Angela Tomkins Dorota Ujma Debra Wale Caitlin Walker

£25.00 (paperback) | 234 x 156mm | 2009 | 208 pp | ISBN 978–1–903152–24–9

Enhancing Graduate Employability
in Business and Management Hospitality Leisure Sport and Tourism

Edited by Nina Becket and Patsy Kemp

E mployability is an important theme for all higher education institutions. This book will be of value to anyone interested in employability, or involved in curriculum development in higher education. The case studies are written by lecturers from the business, hospitality, leisure, sport & tourism communities, and demonstrate best practice in embedding employability into the curriculum.

Contents

Contributors Gillian Armstrong   Karen Bill   Will Bowen-Jones   Nicola Bullivant   John Buswell   Debra Enzenbacher   Lesley Ferkins   Jenny Fleming   Helen George   Kate Greenan   Jacqui Gush   Helen Higson   David Hind   Graham Holden   Marc Keech   Vanessa Knowles   Bridget Major   Mary Malcolm   Una McMahon-Beattie   Angela Maher   Gudrun Myers   Etta Parkes   Petia Petrova   Sean Power   Gail Thompson   Angela Tomkins   Rob Ward   Dorota Ujma

£29.00 (paperback)   246 x 189mm   2006   176 pp   ISBN 1–903152–15–7